pavel feinstein

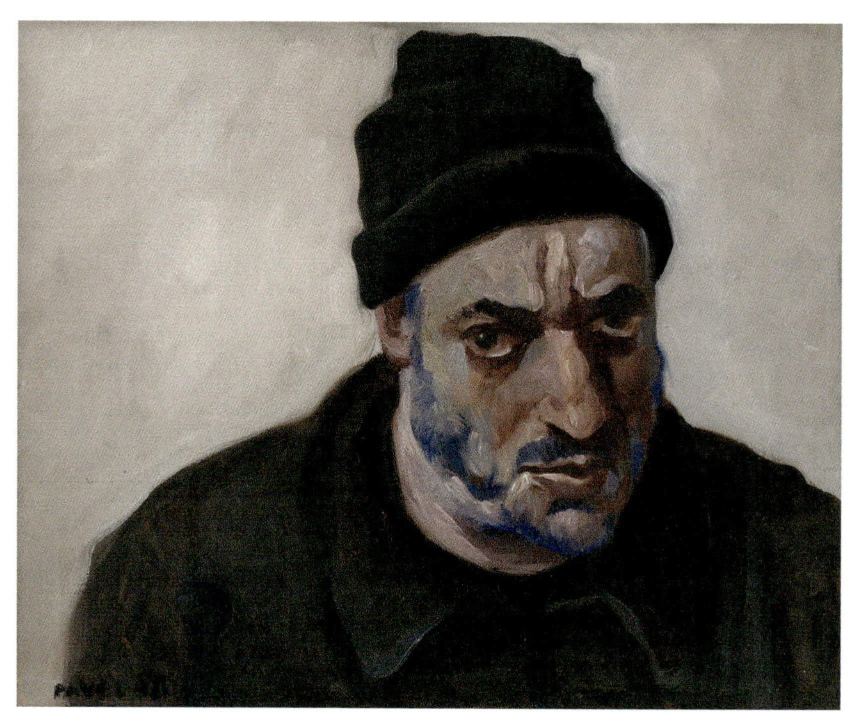

pavel feinstein

les petits fours – das kleine Format / the small format

HIRMER

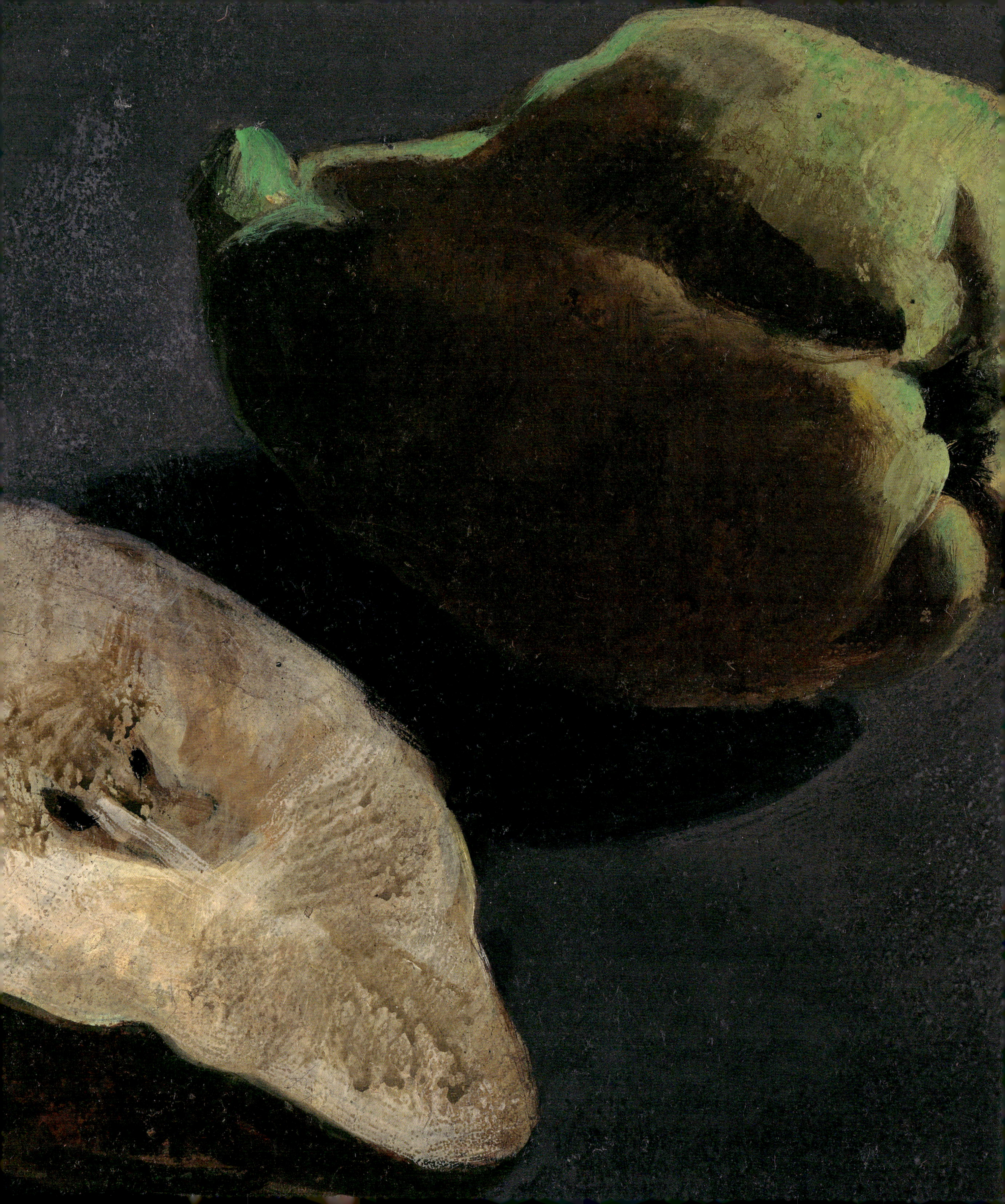

Meinem kunstsinnigen Freund
Vladimir Sichov gewidmet

Dedicated to my art-loving
friend Vladimir Sichov

Stillleben von Pavel Feinstein

Die Malerei von Pavel Feinstein wirkt auf den ersten Blick traditionell und wurde häufig als altmeisterlich beschrieben – der Künstler sei der »neue Altmeister«, schrieb der Kritiker Manfred Schwarz am 7. September 2010 in der *Zeit*. Feinstein bezeugt in seiner Malerei, was er gesehen hat, sein zentrales Thema ist die Welt, wie er sie gefiltert durch sein Temperament sieht. Er arbeitet in den traditionellen Genres von Porträt, Landschaft, Allegorie / Historie und Stillleben.

In seinen Stillleben wird wohl am klarsten, was seine Malerei insgesamt auszeichnet, denn hier ist das Thema so beiläufig und anspruchslos, dass die Malerei als Malerei zum Schwerpunkt der Aufmerksamkeit wird. 1916 stellte der Maler Max Liebermann fest: »Der Satz, dass die gutgemalte Rübe besser sei als die schlechtgemalte Madonna, gehört zum eisernen Bestand der modernen Ästhetik. Aber der Satz ist falsch; er müsste lauten: die gutgemalte Rübe ist ebenso gut wie die gutgemalte Madonna.« Einige Zeilen später zieht er das Fazit: »Der spezifisch malerische Gehalt eines Bildes ist umso größer, je geringer das Interesse an seinem Gegenstande selber ist; je restloser der Inhalt eines Bildes in malerischer Form aufgegangen ist, desto größer ist der Maler.«* Gerade im Stillleben erweist sich die Wahrheit von Liebermanns Feststellung, das zeigen schon die allerfrühesten Bilder dieser Gattung von Jacopo de'Barbari und Michelangelo da Caravaggio. Das Stillleben etablierte sich als selbstständige Gattung, weil es den Malern am ehesten ermöglichte, Malerei als Malerei zu betreiben, ohne auf die Thematik zu viel Rücksicht nehmen zu müssen.

Feinsteins motivisch so karge wie malerisch überschwängliche kleine Stillleben gehören in eine Reihe von Werken großer Maler wie Sánchez Cotán, Chardin, Cézanne, Van Gogh, Schuch, Morandi oder Hockney – oder auch den fotografischen

Pavel Feinstein's Still Lifes

Pavel Feinstein's way of painting appears at first glance to be traditional and has often been described as old-masterly – the artist is the "new Old Master", as critic Manfred Schwarz wrote in "Die Zeit" on September 7th, 2010. Feinstein, in his painting, bears witness to what he has seen; his main subject is the world, as he sees it, filtered through his temperament. He works in the traditional genres of portrait, landscape, allegory / history and still life.

What makes his painting special is best seen in his still lifes, as here the subject is so parenthetical and unassuming that painting itself becomes the centre of attention. In 1916 the painter Max Liebermann said: "The phrase that the well-painted turnip is better than the badly painted Madonna is at the core of modern aesthetics. But it is false; one would have to say that the well-painted turnip is as good as the well-painted Madonna." A few lines later he draws the conclusion: "The specifically painterly content of an image is all the greater, the smaller the interest in its subject matter; the more completely the subject matter of an image is merged with painterly form, the greater the painter."* It is especially in the still lifes that the truth of Liebermann's statement is proven, and indeed is already shown in the very earliest pictures of this genre by Jacopo de' Barbari and Michelangelo da Caravaggio. Still lifes became a genre of their own because they best enabled painters to pursue painting as painting, without taking into account much of the subject matter.

Feinstein's still lifes, skimpy in motif but exuberantly painted, stand in line with a number of works by great painters such as Sánchez Cotán, Chardin, Cézanne, van Gogh, Schuch, Morandi or Hockney – or the photographic still lifes of an artist like Wols. The objects in Feinstein's paintings are presented in a neutral, mostly brown-grey space. They

Stillleben eines Wols. Feinsteins Bildgegenstände werden in einem neutralen, meist braungrauen Raum präsentiert. Dabei werden sie in einer Malweise dargestellt, die vor Cézanne so nicht möglich gewesen wäre – sie sind nicht kleinmeisterlich oder fotorealistisch und zentralperspektivisch ausgeführt, sondern in einer souveränen Handschrift, die sich aus großer Entfernung noch klar lesen lässt. (David Hockney hat zu Recht erklärt, dass Cézanne der Erste war, der seine Bilder mit zwei gleichzeitig geöffneten Augen malte, die Zentralperspektive dadurch vermied und einen malerischen Reichtum erschloss, von dem nach ihm zahllose Maler profitieren konnten. Feinstein ist einer davon.) Bei extremer Nahsicht lösen sich die Bildgegenstände in einer sinnlichen, gestischen, reinen Malerei auf. Feinstein stellt so eine enge Verbindung zwischen Betrachter, Bild und Maler her, denn im Nachvollzug der malerischen Handschrift kann der Betrachter immer wieder neu die Entstehung des Bildes mit den auf ihm dargestellten Gegenständen erleben. So ereignet sich der künstlerische Schöpfungsakt jedesmal neu, und die Bilder bleiben zeitgenössisch frisch. Die Gegenstände sind nur selten historisch bestimmbar, denn es sind überwiegend nachwachsende Naturprodukte oder im Falle der Porzellangefäße und Gläser so allgemeine Formen, wie es sie seit mindestens 100 Jahren gibt. Ganz selten finden sich Indizien für die jüngste Vergangenheit – wir müssen bei figurativen Darstellungen immer von Vergangenheit sprechen, denn der Maler bezeugt etwas, das er gesehen und geschildert hat. Die Malerei handelt davon, die Erinnerung an diesen Moment in die Gegenwart des Betrachters zu versetzen, die Vergangenheit also zu aktualisieren. Ein Beispiel für einen näher bestimmbaren historischen Moment liefert das Hühnerei, auf dem der Produktionsstempel zu erkennen ist, mit dem die Agrarbürokratie der EU die Bauern erst seit gut 15 Jahren drangsaliert. Morandi oder Cézanne hätten das so nicht sehen können. Hockneys Evian-Flaschen auf seinen Stillleben von Mitte der 1990er Jahre sind ein Parallelphänomen zu Feinsteins Hühnerei.

are presented in a pictorial manner impossible in the times before Cézanne; they are not painted in the manner of the lesser masters or photo-realistically, but in a self-confident hand, still readable from a great distance. (David Hockney was right when he declared that Cézanne had been the first to paint his pictures with both eyes open simultaneously, thus eschewing central perspective and opening up a painterly richness that countless painters after him were able to profit from. Feinstein is one of them.) Seen from an extremely short distance, the pictorial objects dissolve into a sensual and gestural, pure way of painting. Thus Feinstein establishes a close relationship between the viewer, the image and the painter, as in recreating the painterly hand the viewer can, every time, experience again the origin of the image with its depicted objects. So the act of artistic creation is repeated every time and the images remain contemporary and fresh. Seldom are the objects historically describable, as we mostly deal with regrowing natural products or, in the case of the porcelain pots and glasses, forms so common that we have known them for a century or more. Very rarely are there indications of the recent past; we have to speak about the past when dealing with figuration as the painter testifies something he has seen and portrayed. Painting is about putting the reminiscence of that moment into the presence of the viewer, that is, bringing the past up to date. An example for a definable historical moment is the hen's egg on which you can discern the production stamp with which the agricultural bureaucracy of the EU has been bullying farmers only for the past 15 years. Morandi or Cézanne would not have been able to see that this way. Hockney's Evian bottles in still lifes from the middle of the 1990s are a parallel phenomenon to Feinstein's hen's eggs.

Pavel Feinstein paints fruits, cheese, eggs, fish and meat, presented on crockery and complete with cutlery. Sometimes paint tubes give away the location of the origin of the paintings – a painter's studio. Feinstein's arrangements make it clear that his paintings are about colours and their at most inspiring effect. The pried-open pomegranates show, in

Pavel Feinstein malt Obst, Käse, Eier, Fisch und Fleisch, präsentiert auf Geschirr und mit Besteck. Manchmal geben Farbtuben einen Hinweis auf den Entstehungsort der Bilder – ein Maleratelier. Feinsteins Arrangements verdeutlichen, dass es in seinen Bildern um Farben und ihre möglichst inspirierende Wirkung geht. Die aufgebrochenen Granatäpfel zeigen kontrastierend zur weißlichen Schalenhaut ein tief leuchtendes Rot, die geschälten Orangen eben Orange, die Garnelen Lachsorange, Blau holt sich der Maler vom chinesischen Porzellan usw. Eine Schale mit elf Datteln demonstriert, was Kandinsky mit »Punkt und Linie zu Fläche« für ein flexibles Kompositionsmodell entworfen hat. Diese kleinen Gemälde stehen autonom und sehr lebendig jeweils für sich, als Gruppe gesehen ergeben sie dazu noch eine besonders eindringliche Meta-Komposition. Die raffinierten Anschnitte seiner Bildgegenstände zwingen den Betrachter, über den Bildrand hinauszugehen und Verbindungen zu den anderen Bildern herzustellen. Die Ausschnitte dynamisieren das Sehen, halten die Augen des Betrachters in Bewegung. (Nur Tote bewegen sich nicht.) Pavel Feinsteins Malerei feiert das Leben.

Welches Temperament liegt hinter diesen außerordentlichen kleinen Bildern, was macht sie unverwechselbar und zwingend notwendig? Feinsteins Bilder sind weder so asketisch wie Morandi noch so sonnig wie Van Gogh, noch so knallbunt vergnügt wie Hockney – sie sind sinnlich, auf einer melancholischen Grundlage. Der englische Ausdruck »bittersweet« trifft es am genauesten. So lange es Maler wie Pavel Feinstein gibt, können wir feiern, ohne zu vergessen, wie viel Angst und Leid es in der Welt gibt.

Kay Heymer, Essen, 27. Januar 2015

Anmerkung: * Max Liebermann: *Die Phantasie in der Malerei.* Berlin: Cassirer, 1916, S. 24–26.

contrast to the whitish membrane, a deep shining red; the peeled oranges are just orange, the shrimps are salmon orange, and the blue the painter gets from Chinese porcelain, and so on. A bowl of dates demonstrates the kind of flexible model of composition Kandinsky outlined with "Punkt und Linie zu Fläche" (Point and Line to Plane). These small-sized paintings stand autonomously for themselves in lively manner, so, as a group, they also create a particularly impressive meta-composition. The ingenious sections of his pictorial objects force the viewer to surpass the confines of the painting and establish connections with the other images. The sections give a dynamic quality to seeing, keep the eyes of the beholder in motion. (Only the dead are motionless). Pavel Feinstein's painting celebrates life.

What kind of temperament is behind these extraordinary small-sized paintings; what makes them so distinctive and compelling? Feinstein's paintings are neither as ascetic as Morandi's nor as sunny as van Gogh's, nor as gaudy as Hockney's – they are sensual on a melancholy basis. The English expression "bittersweet" is the closest match. As long as there are painters like Pavel Feinstein, we can celebrate, without forgetting how much fear and pain there is in the world.

Kay Heymer, Essen, January 27th, 2015

Note: * Max Liebermann: *Die Phantasie in der Malerei.* Berlin: Cassirer, 1916, pp. 24–26.

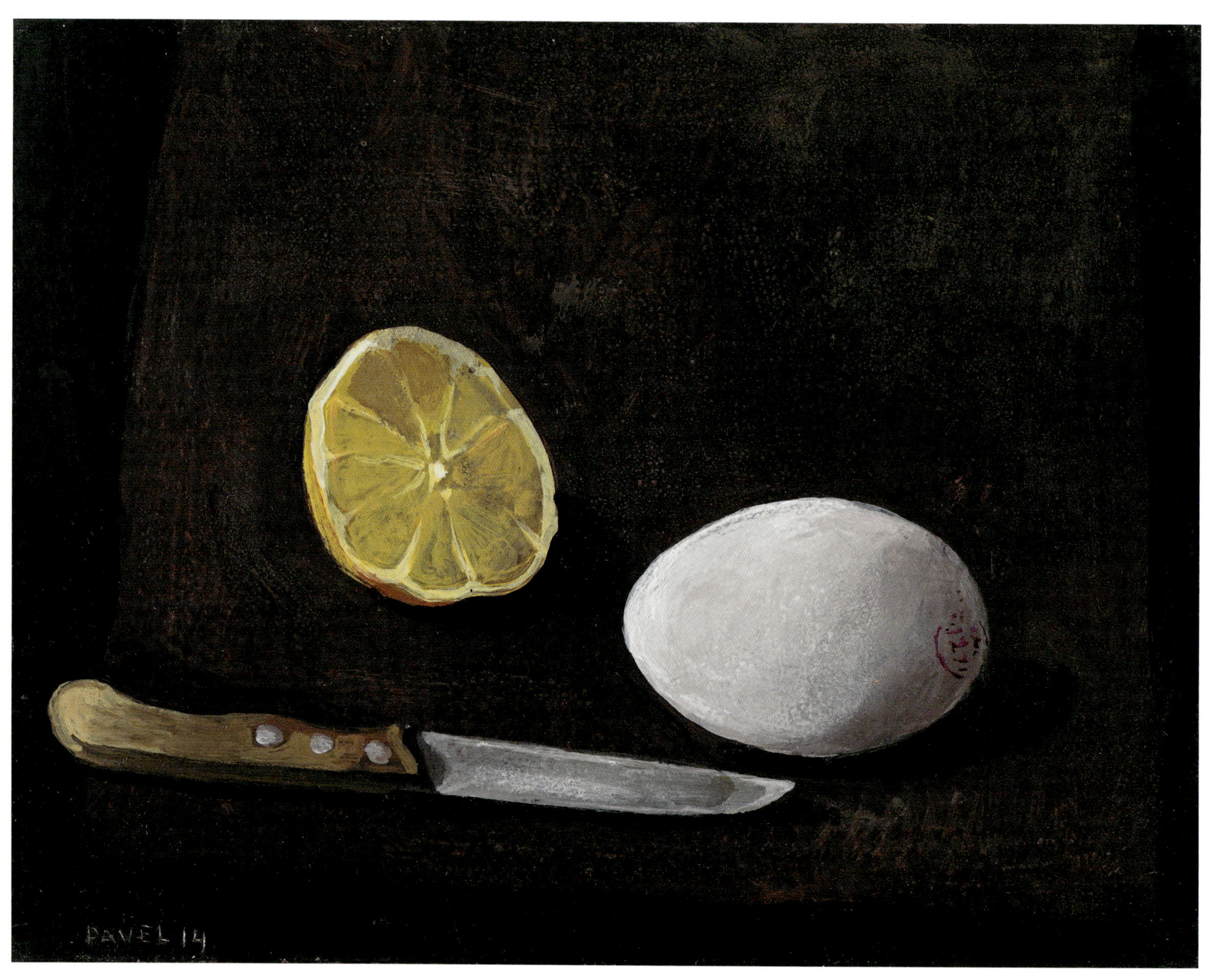

1846, **Tempera auf Hartfaser** / Tempera on hardboard, **24 × 30 cm, 2014**

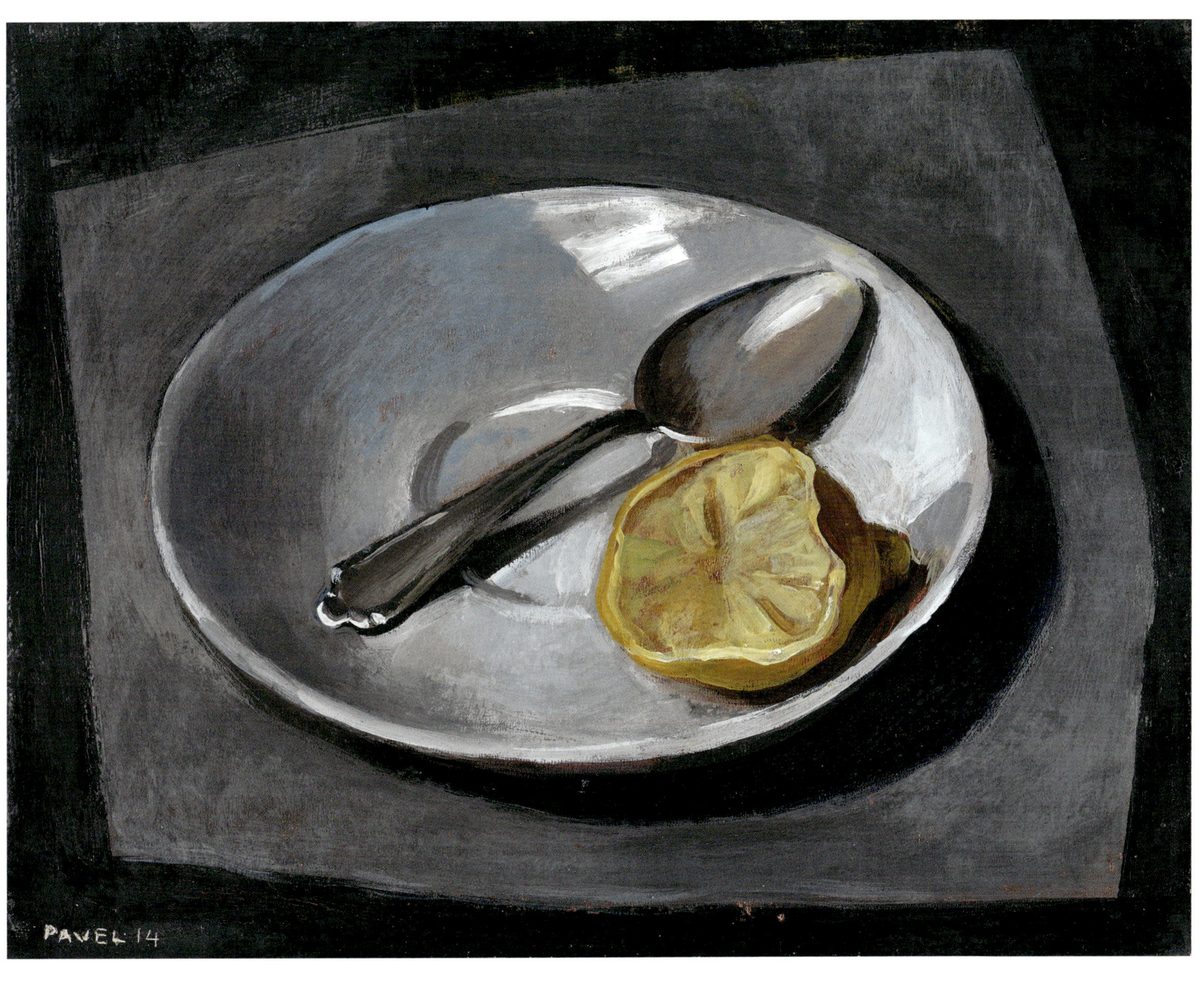

1882, Tempera auf Hartfaser / Tempera on hardboard, 24 × 30 cm, 2014

1886, **Tempera auf Hartfaser** / Tempera on hardboard, 30 × 30 cm, 2014

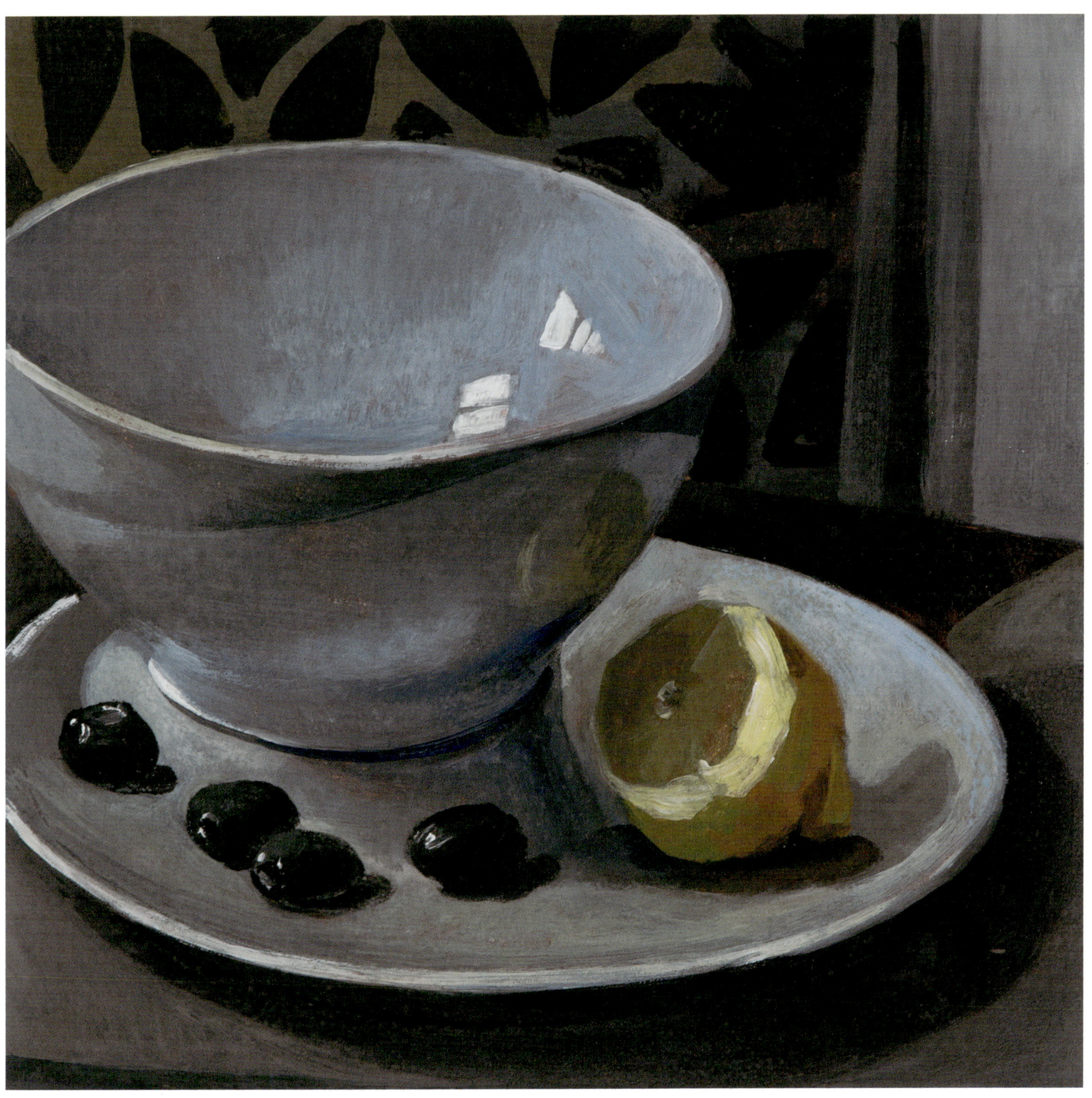

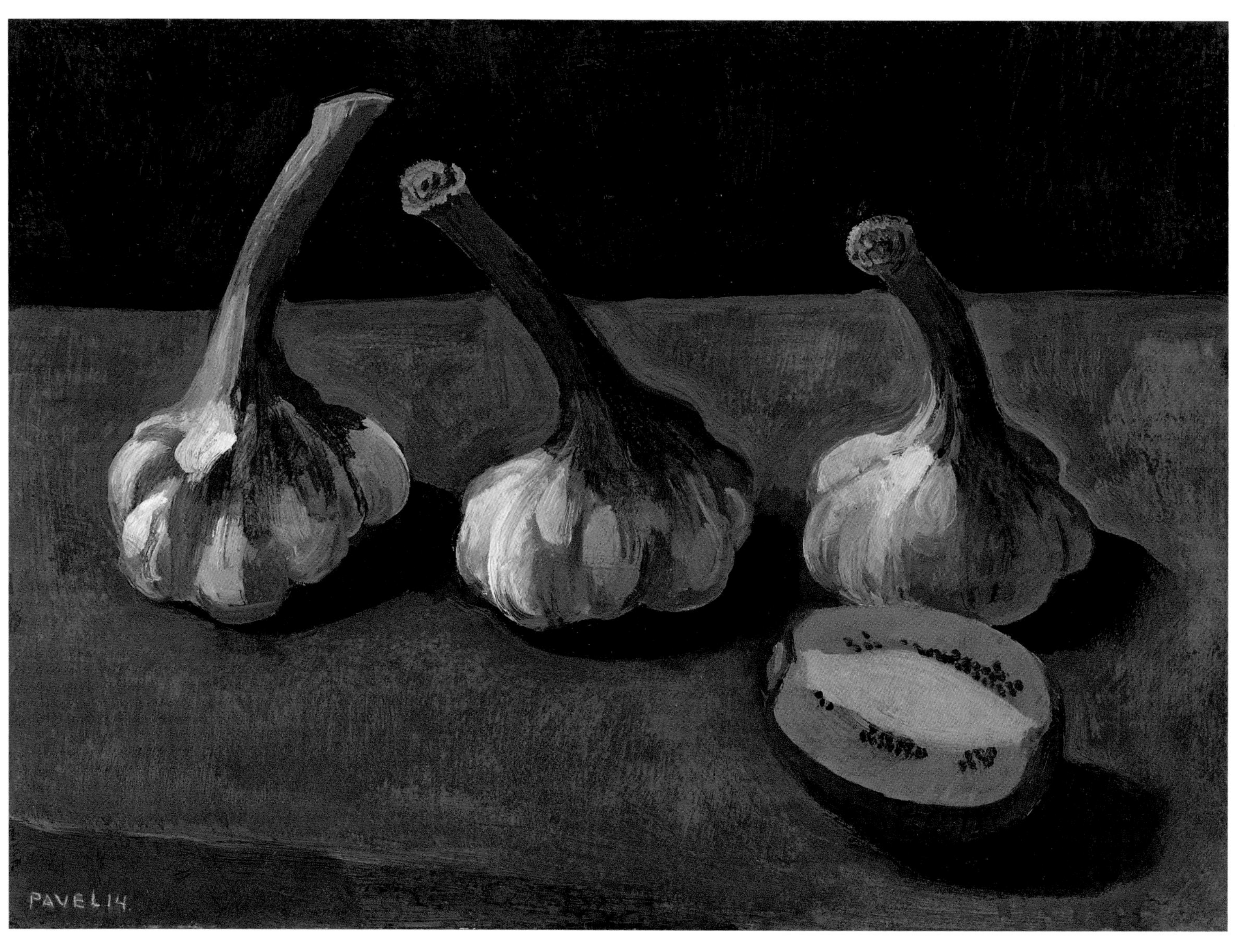

1940, **Tempera auf Hartfaser** / Tempera on hardboard, **30 × 40 cm, 2014**

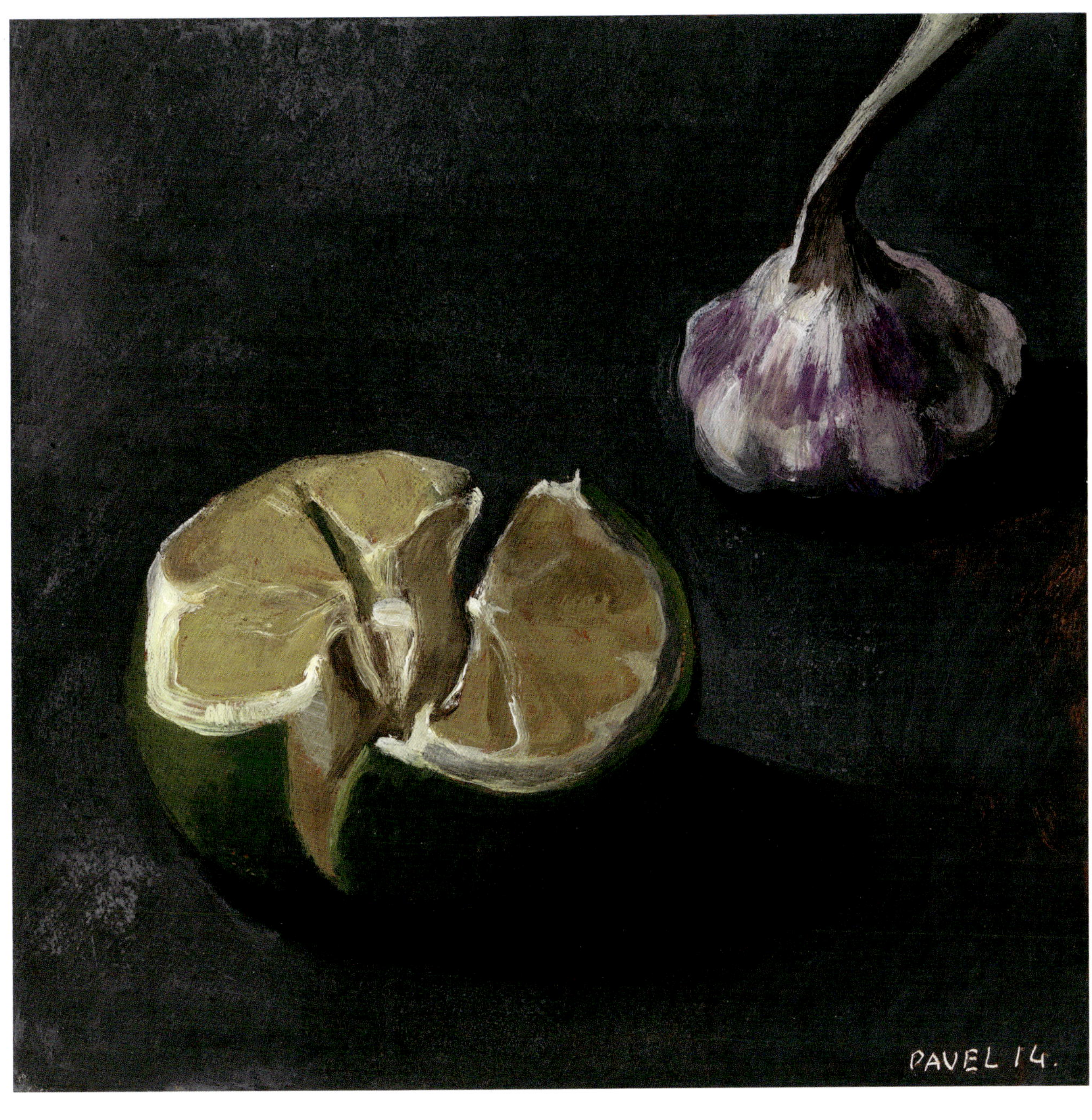

1955, **Tempera auf Hartfaser** / Tempera on hardboard, **30 × 30 cm, 2014**

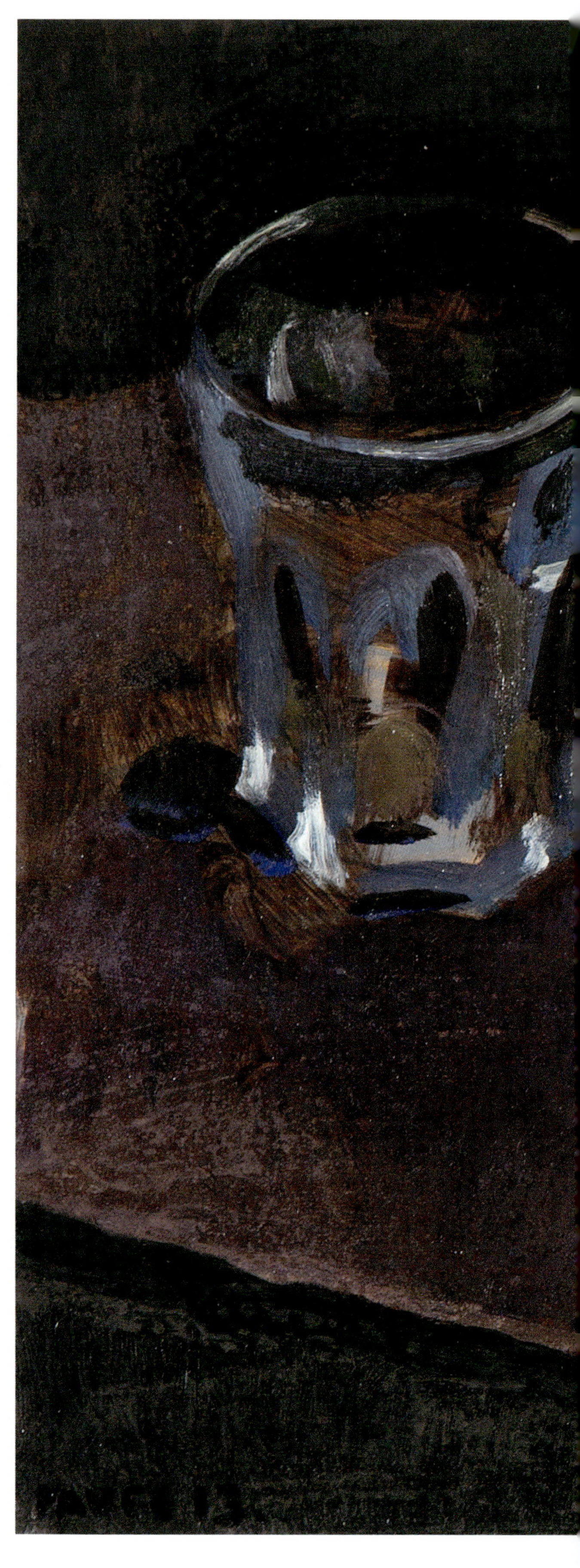

1811, **Tempera auf Hartfaser** / Tempera on hardboard, 30 × 40 cm, 2013

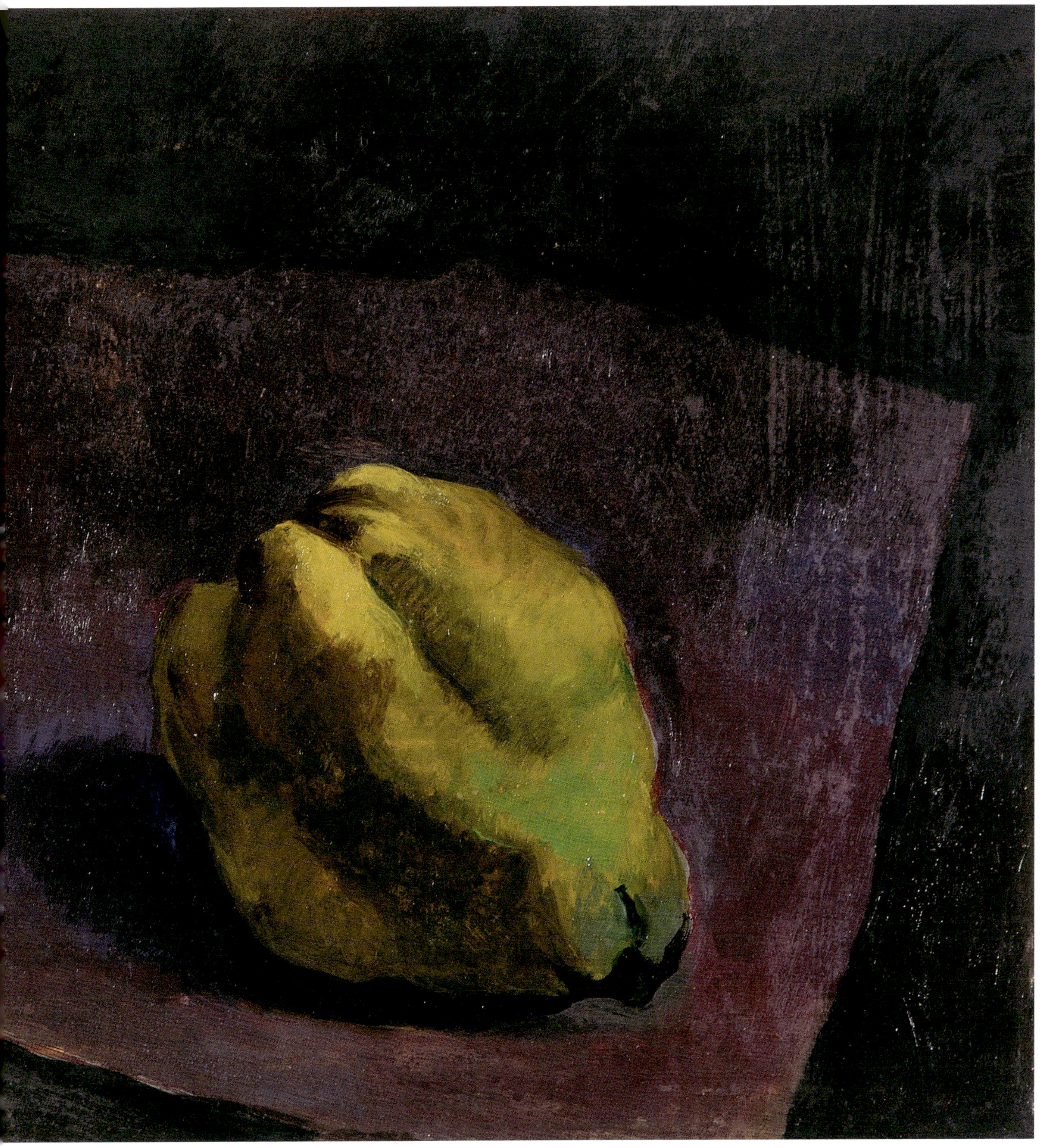

1746, **Tempera auf Hartfaser** / Tempera on hardboard, **40 × 30 cm, 2013**

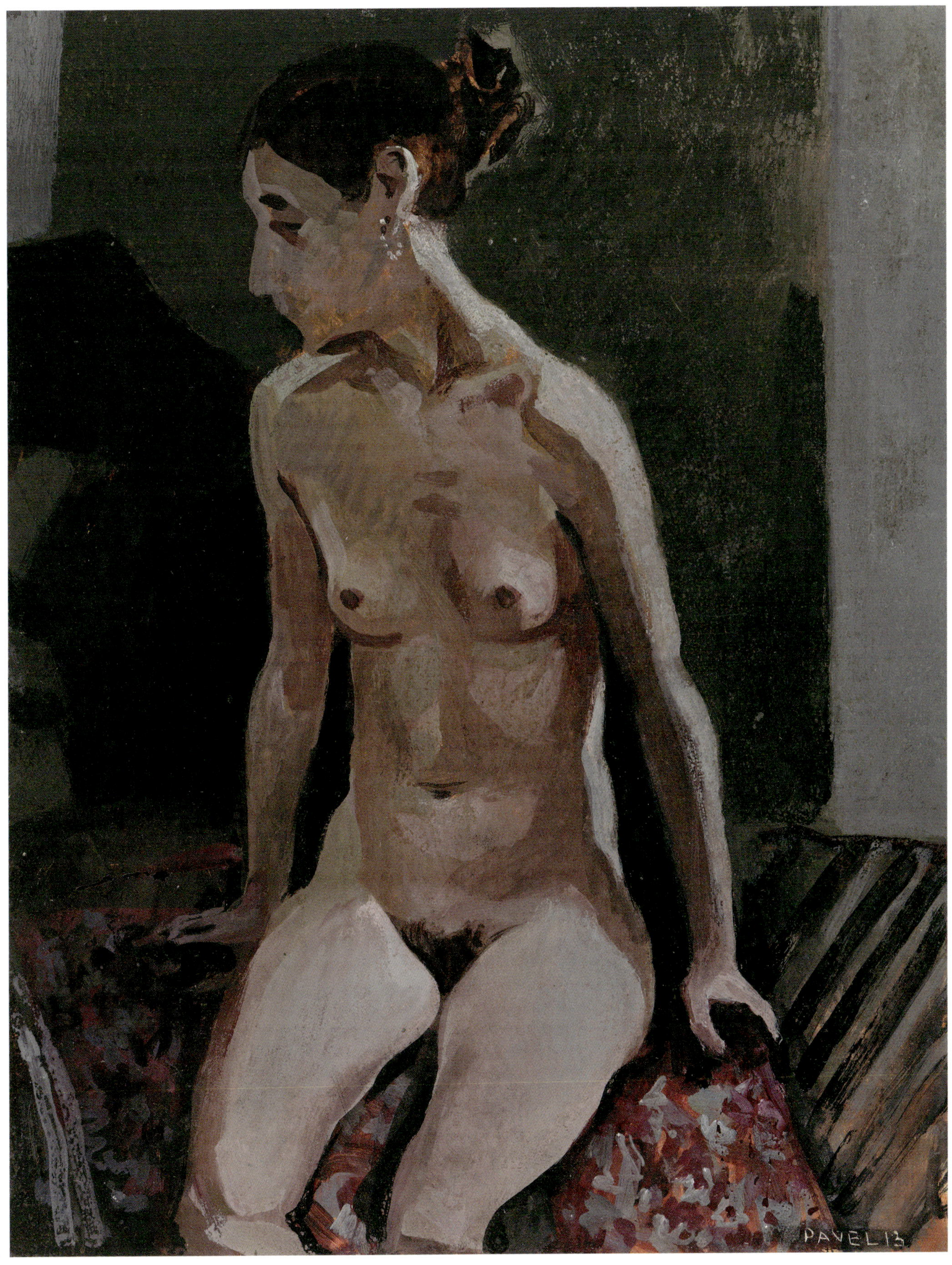
PAVEL 13

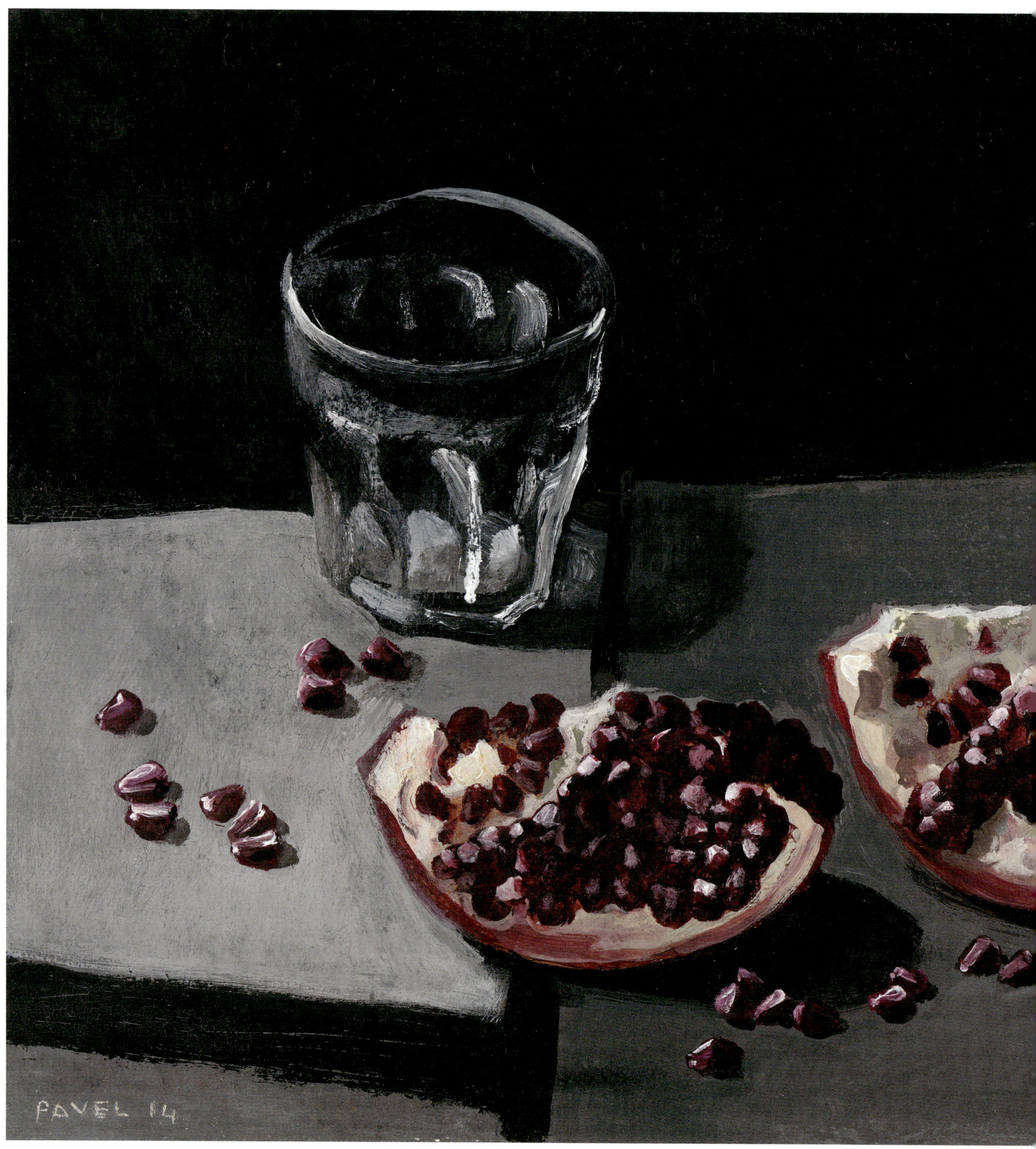
PAVEL 14

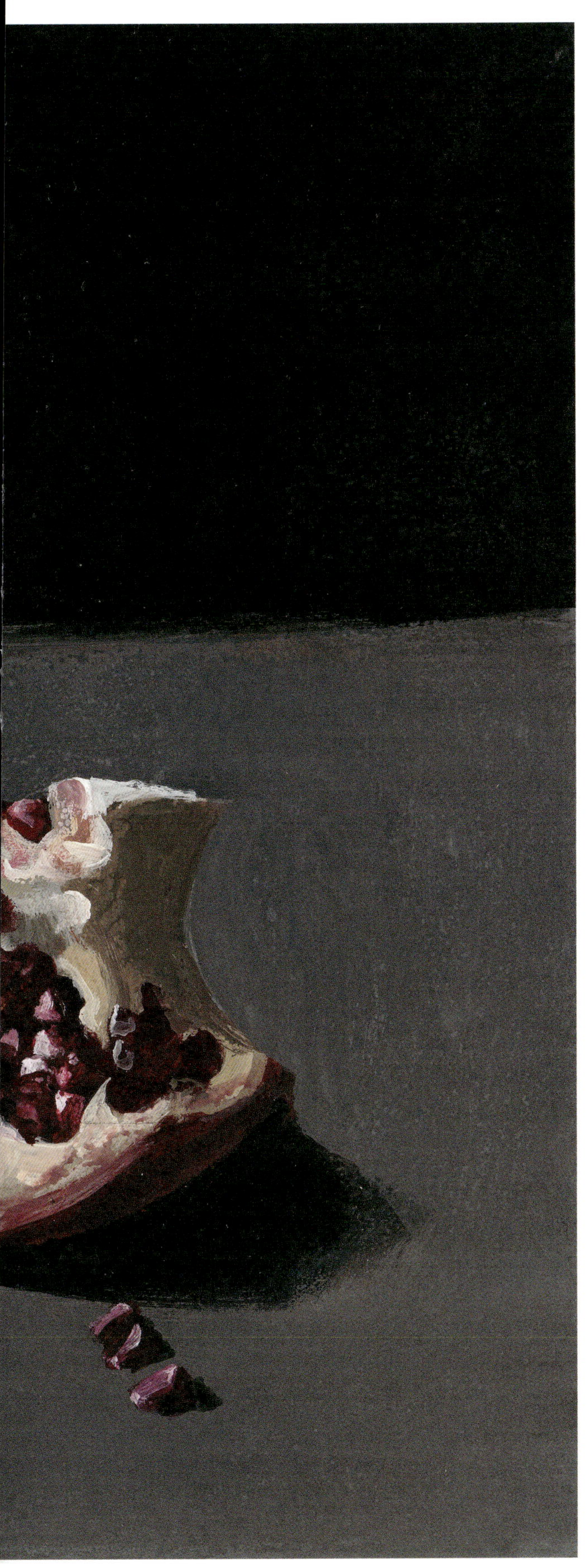

1947, **Tempera auf Hartfaser** / Tempera on hardboard, **30 × 40 cm, 2014**

1827, **Tempera auf Hartfaser** / Tempera on hardboard, 30 × 40 cm, 2013

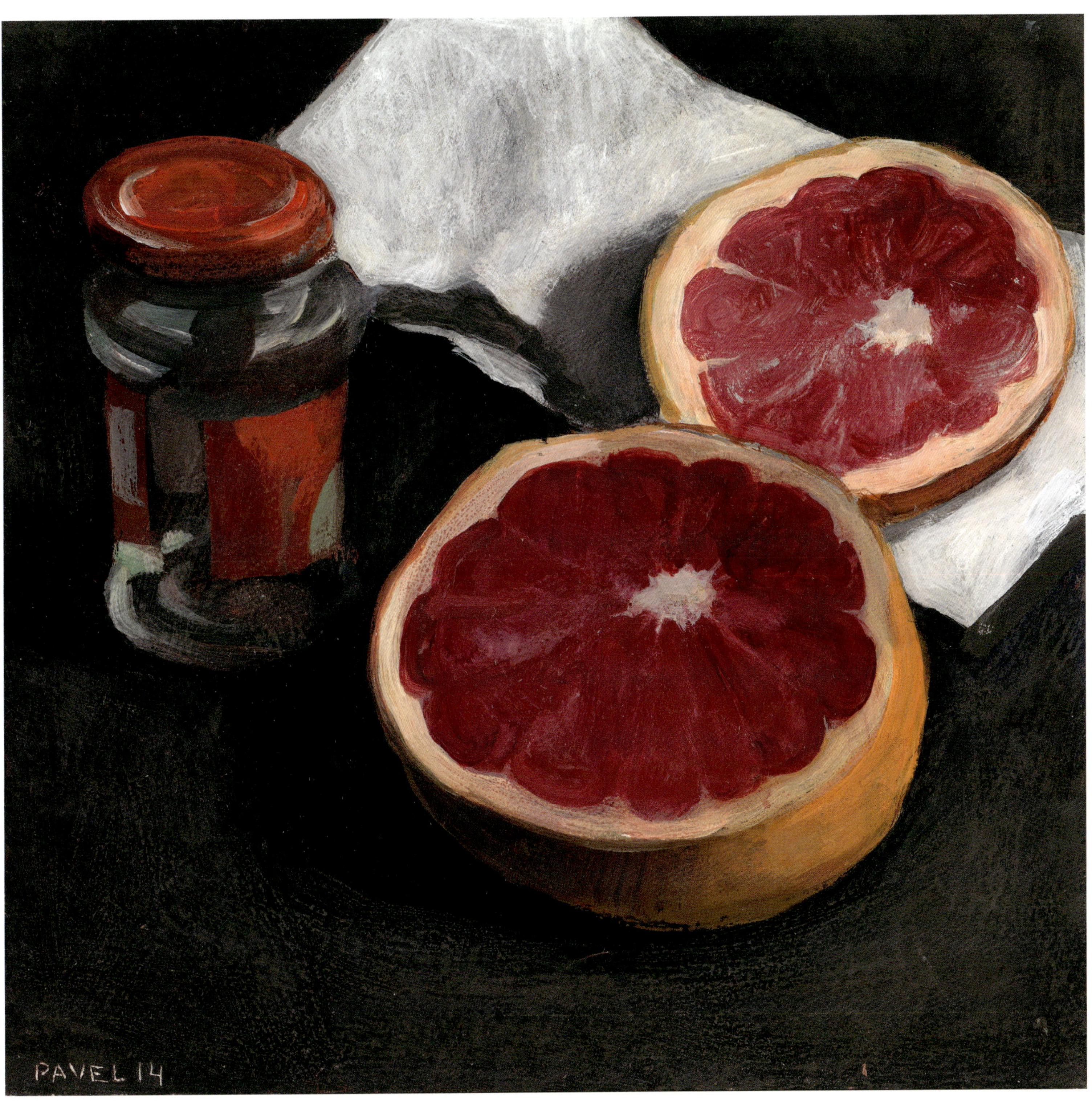
PAVEL 14

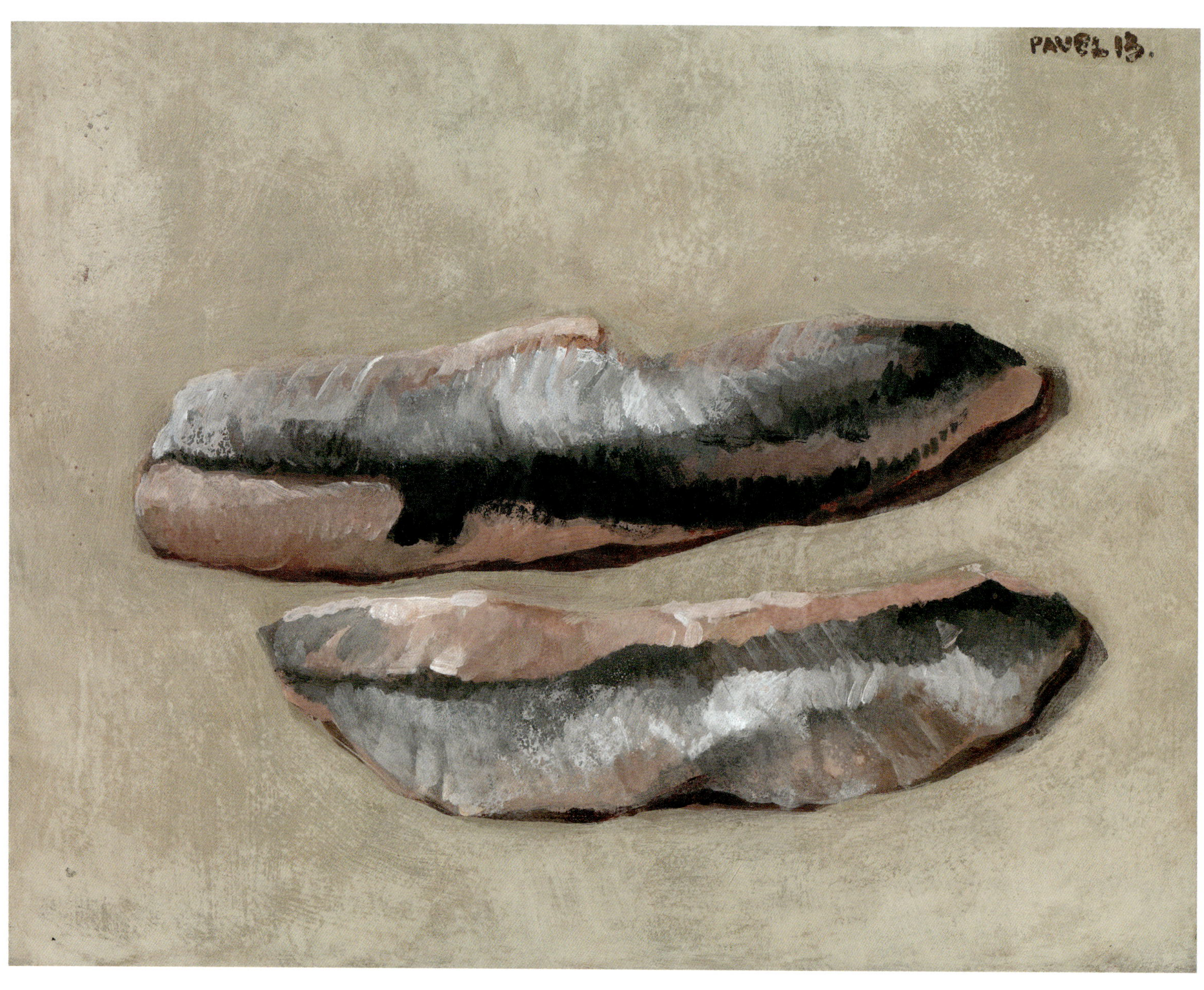

1692, **Tempera auf Hartfaser** / Tempera on hardboard, 24 × 30 cm, 2013

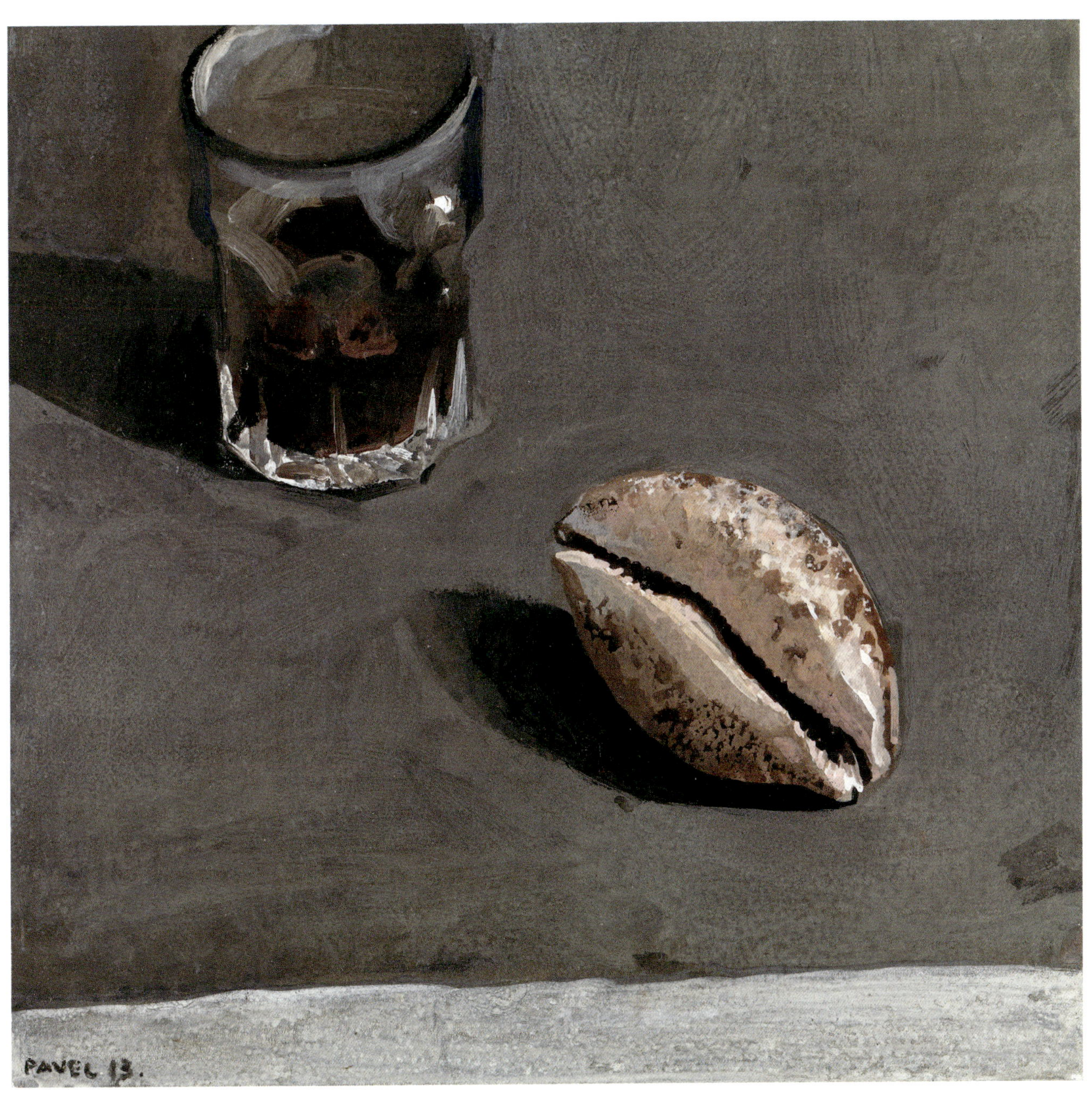

1795, **Tempera auf Hartfaser** / Tempera on hardboard, 30 × 30 cm, 2013

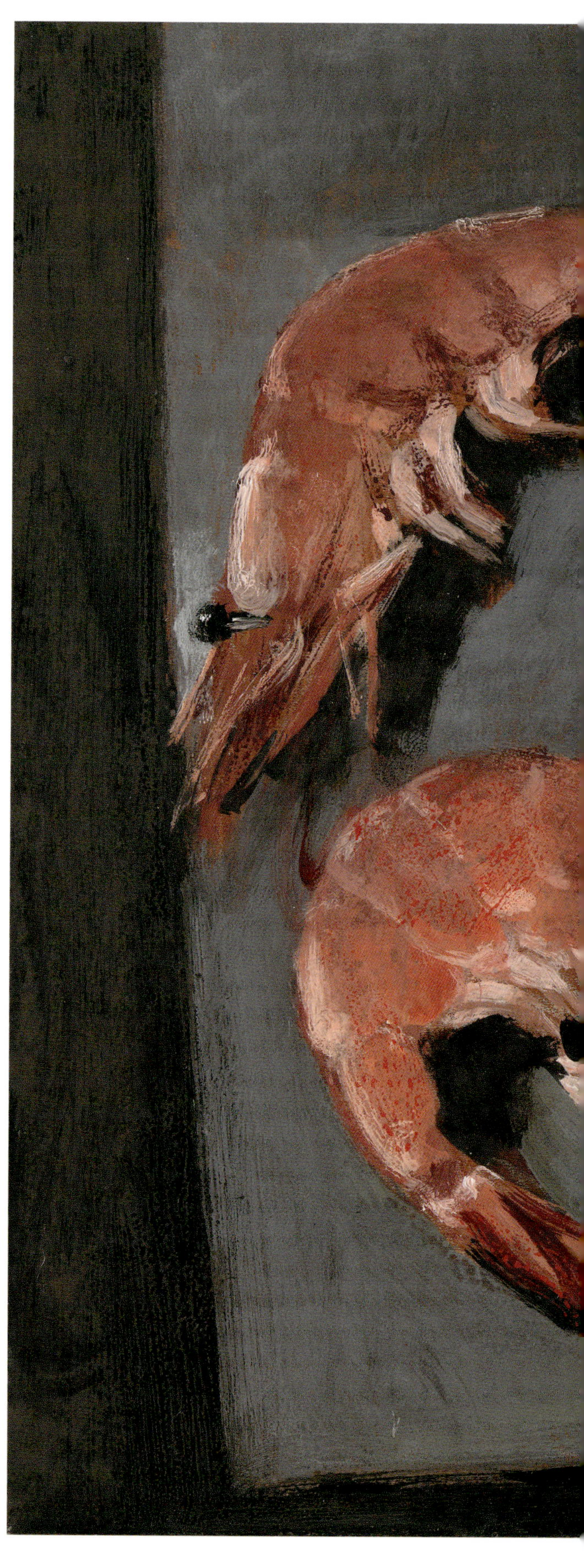

1858, **Tempera auf Hartfaser** / Tempera on hardboard, **24 × 30 cm, 2014**

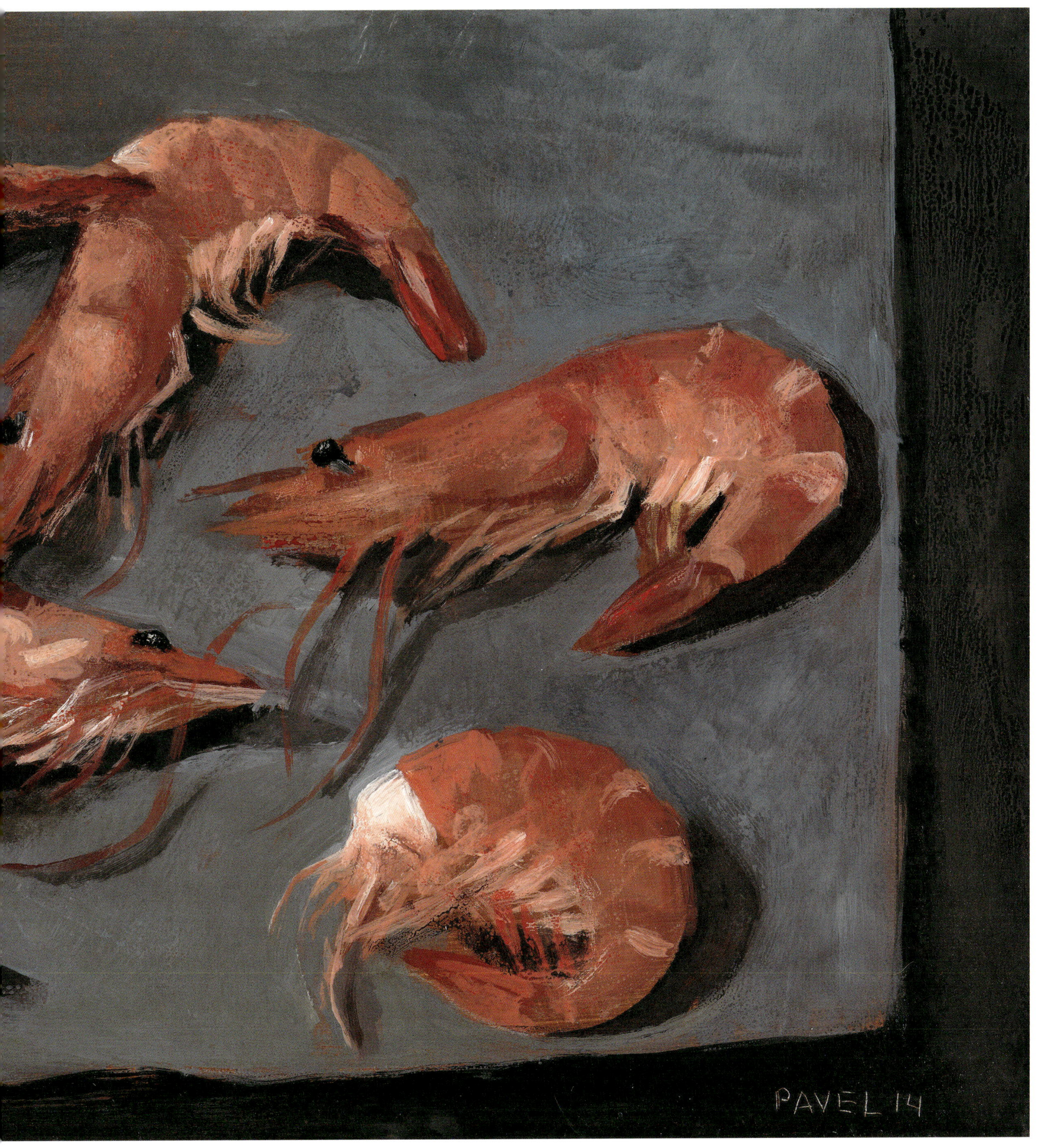
PAVEL 14

***1884*, Tempera auf Hartfaser** / Tempera on hardboard, **24 × 30 cm, 2014**

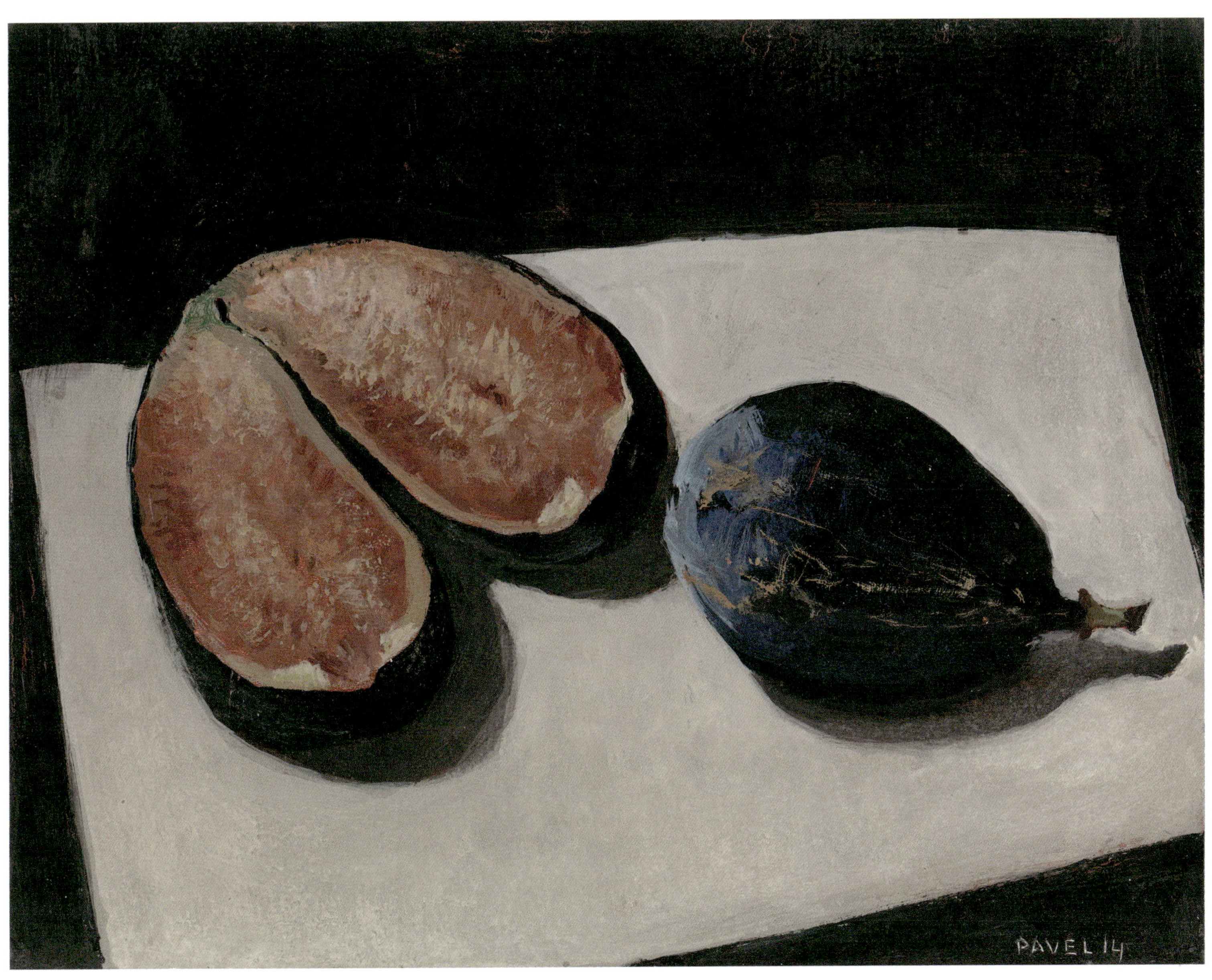
PAVEL 14

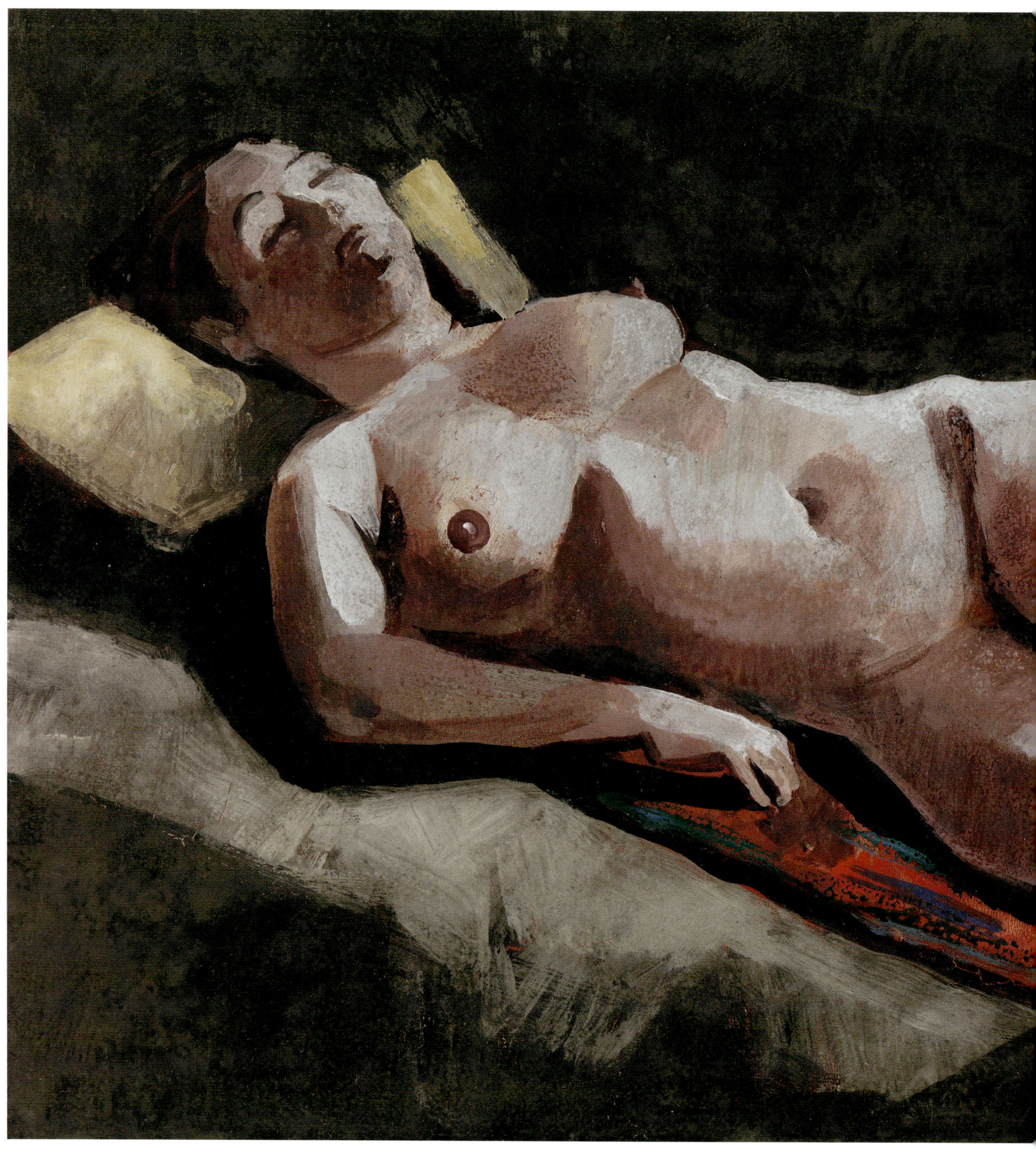

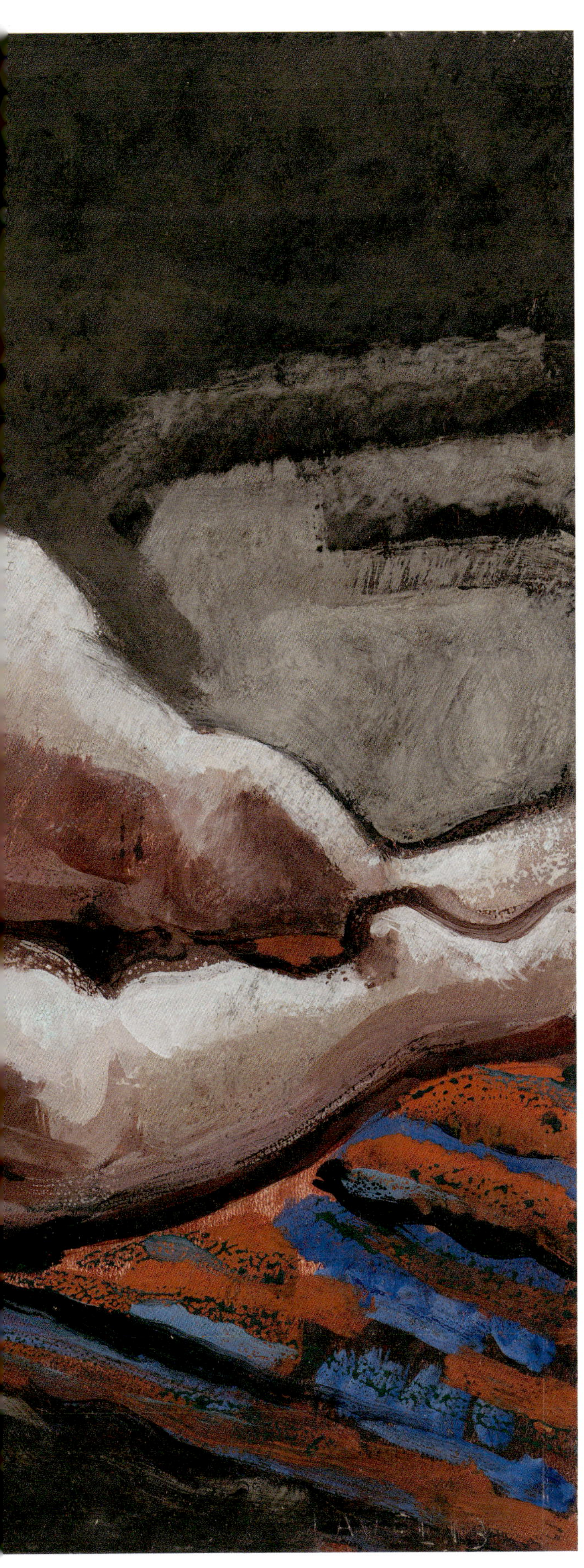

1716, **Tempera auf Hartfaser** / Tempera on hardboard, 30 × 40 cm, 2013

1731, **Tempera auf Hartfaser** / Tempera on hardboard, 30 × 40 cm, 2013

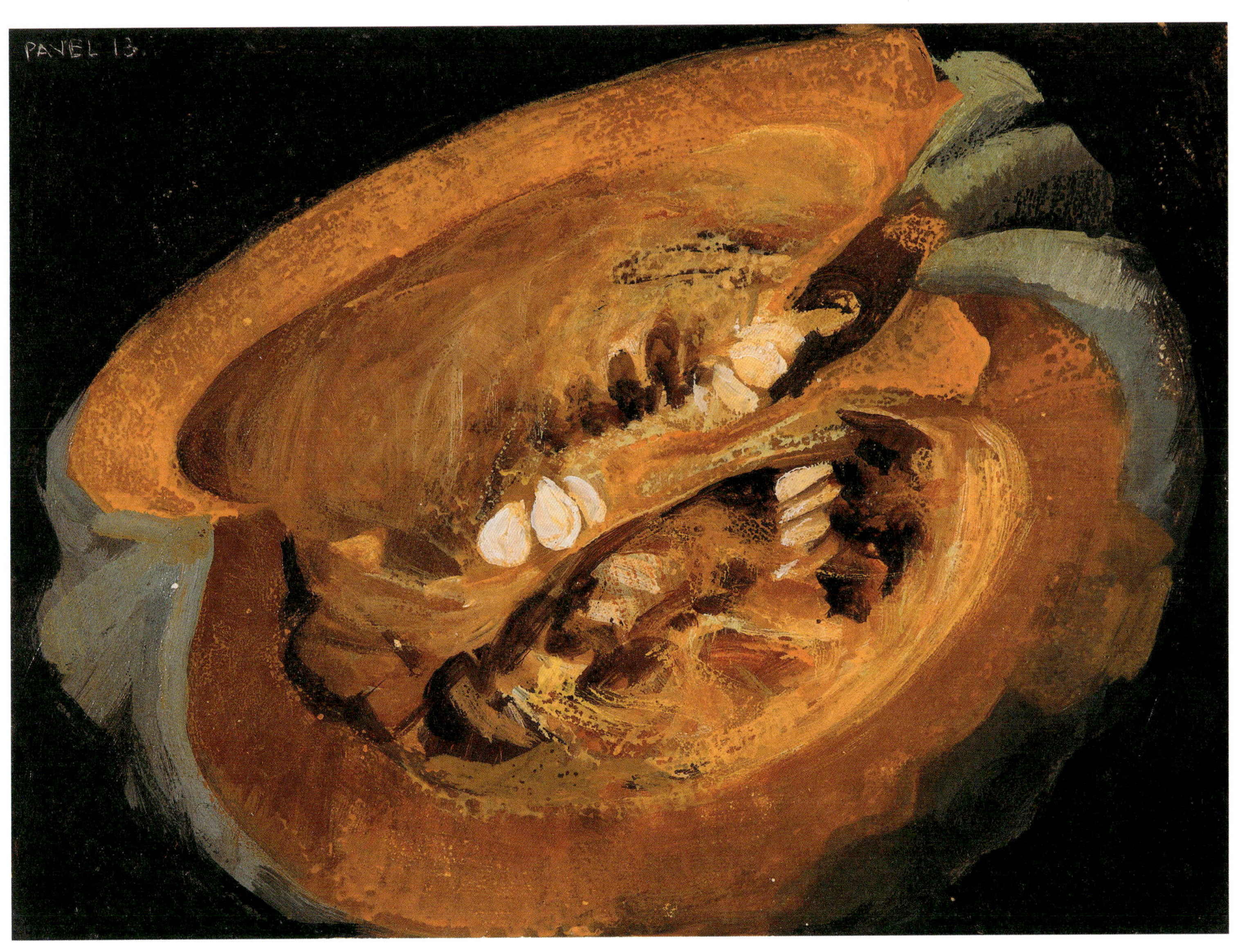
PAVEL 13.

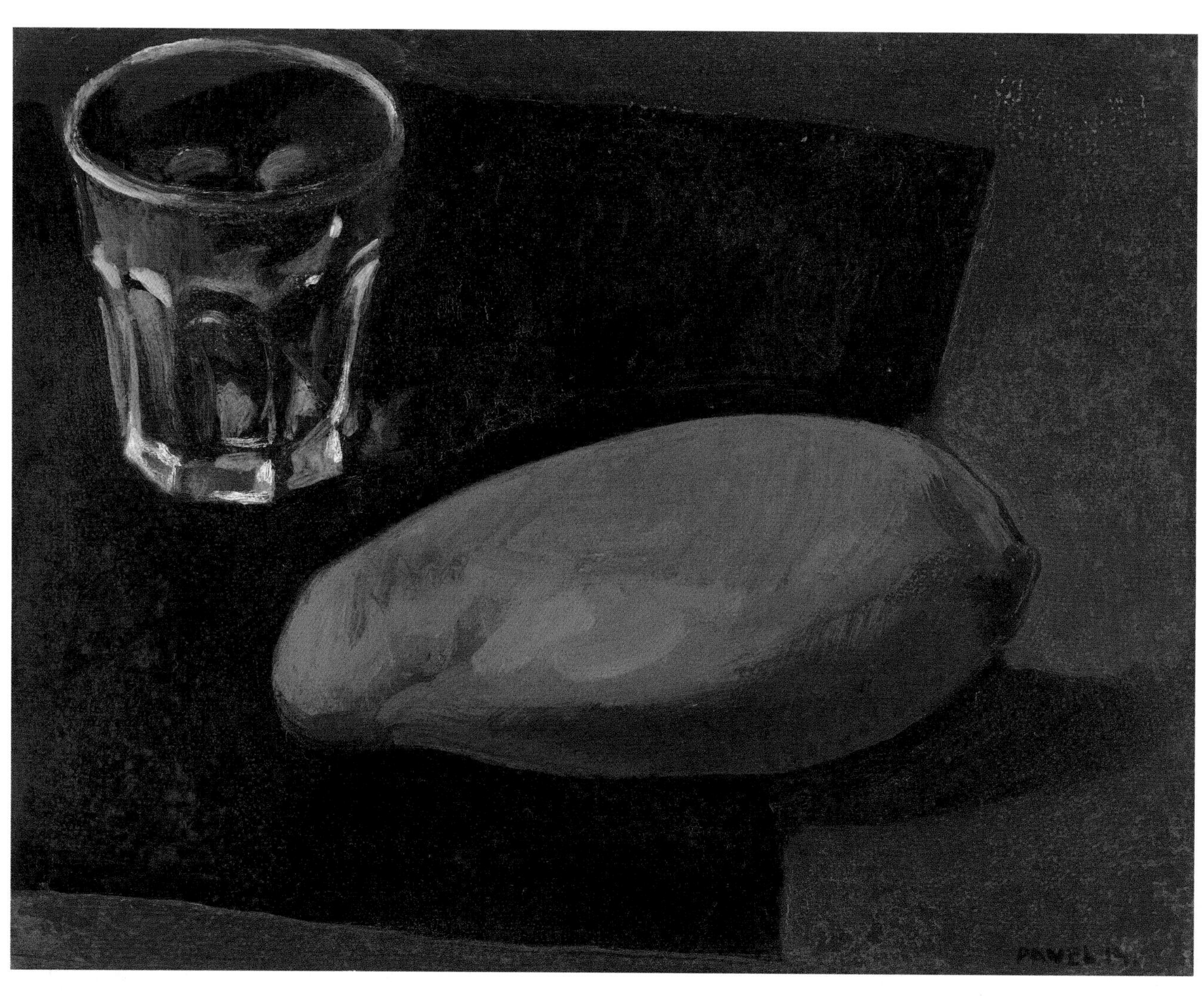

1885, **Tempera auf Hartfaser** / Tempera on hardboard, **24 × 30 cm, 2014**

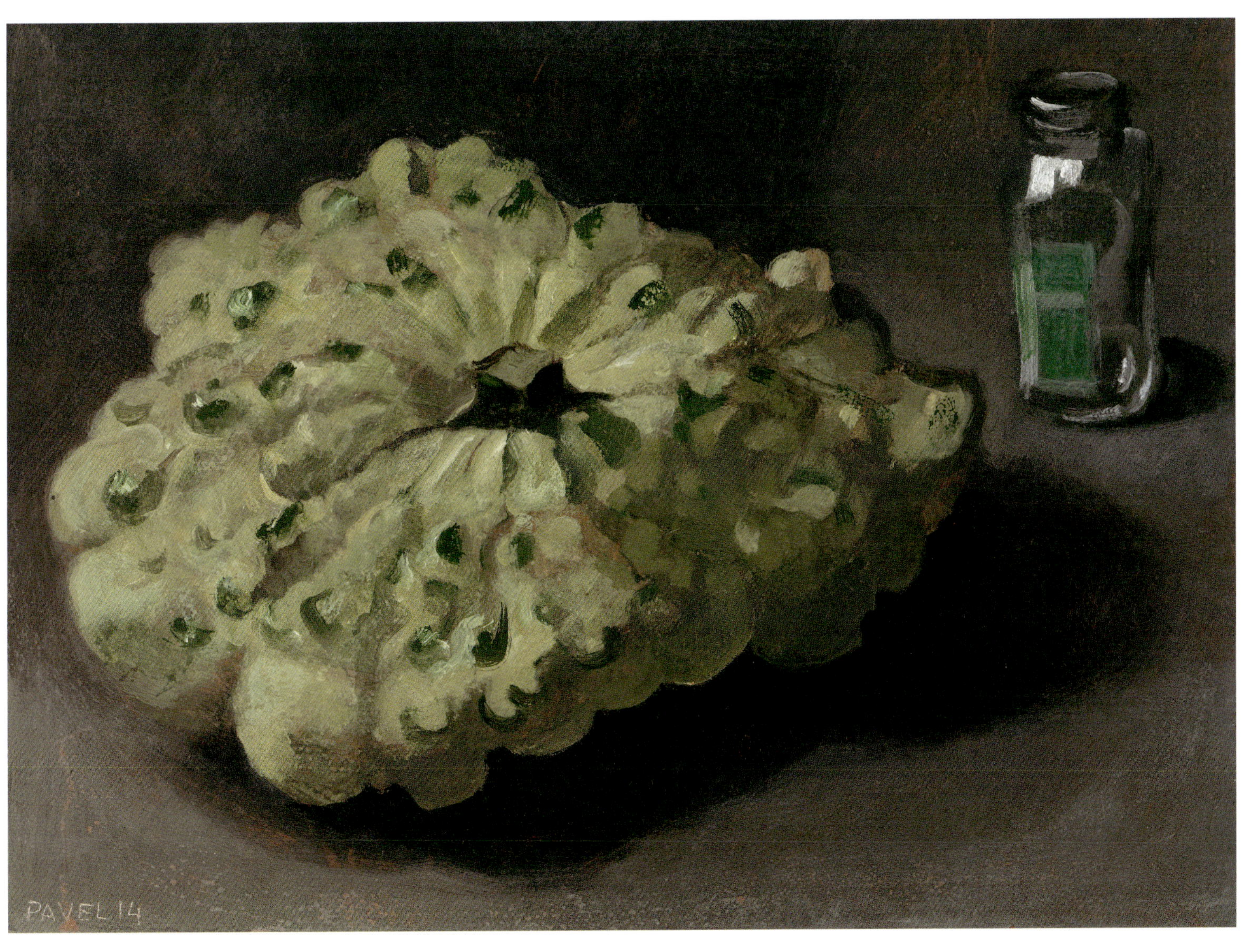

1945, **Tempera auf Hartfaser** / Tempera on hardboard, **30 × 40 cm, 2014**

1802, **Tempera auf Hartfaser** / Tempera on hardboard, 30 × 30 cm, 2013

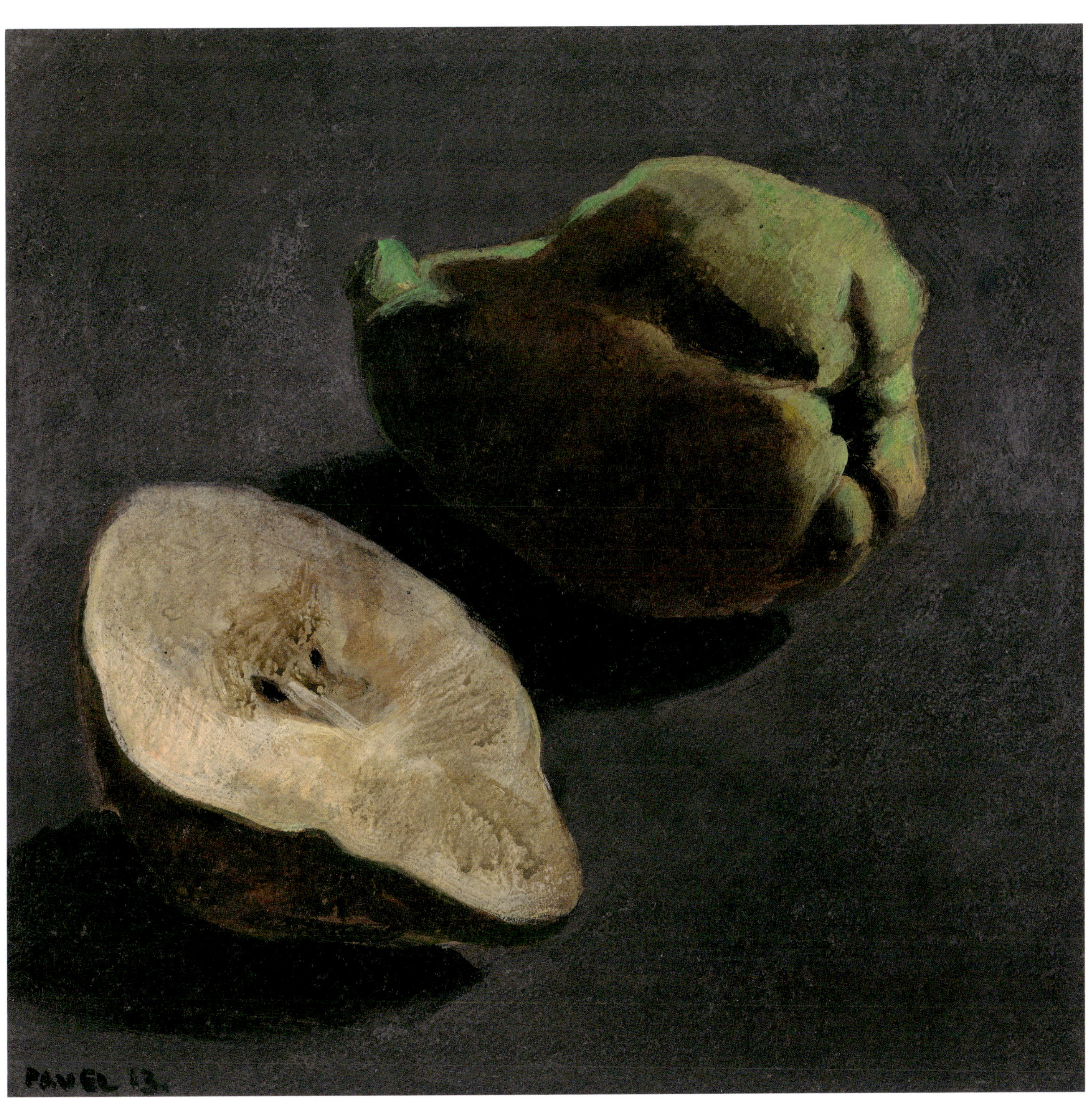
PAVEL 13

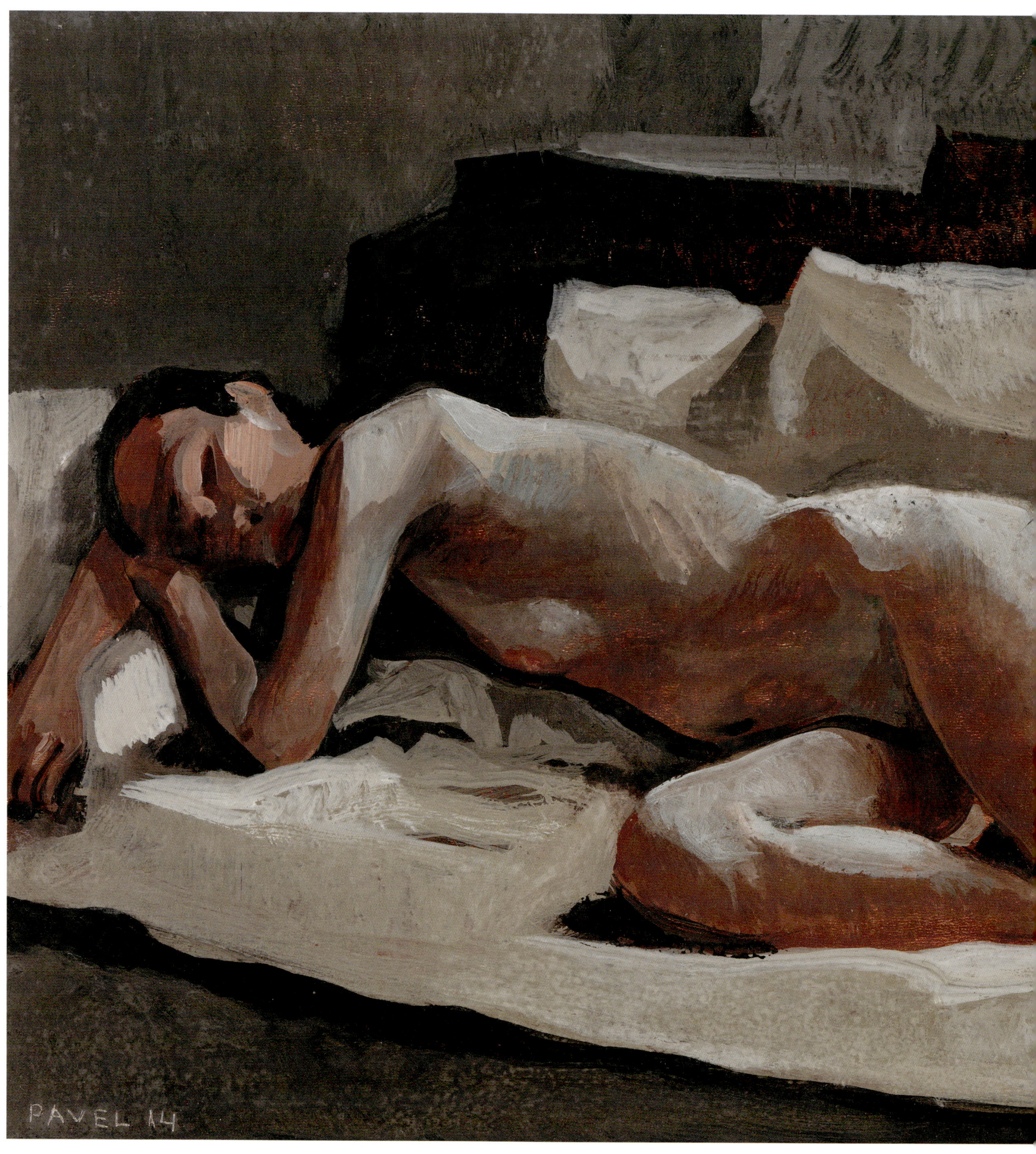
PAVEL 14

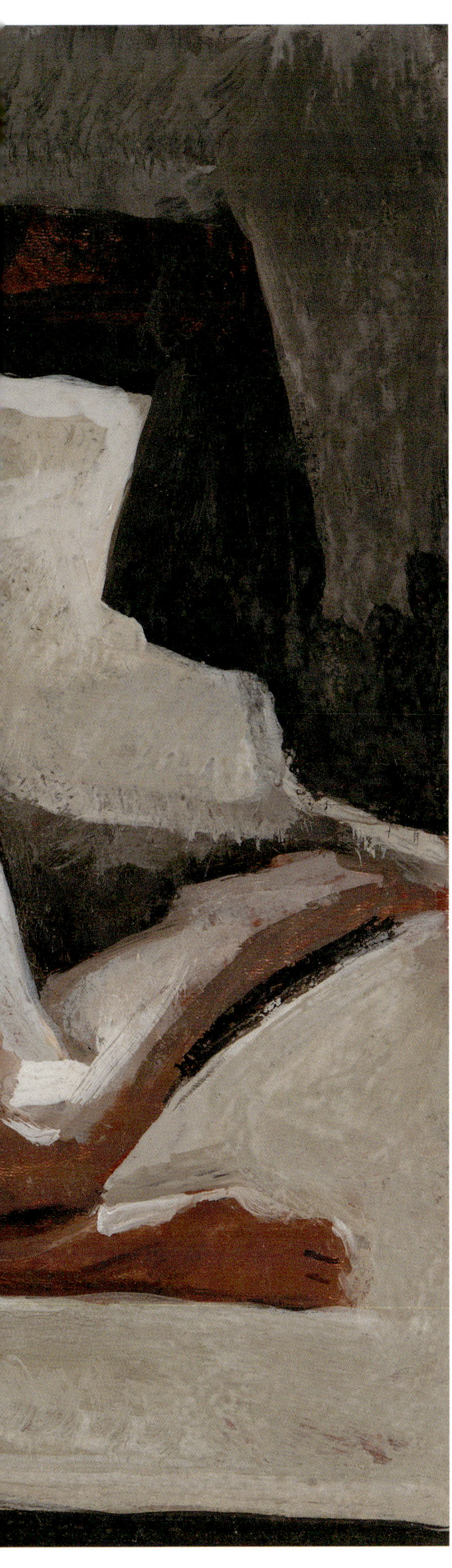

1852, **Tempera auf Hartfaser** / Tempera on hardboard, **24 × 30 cm, 2014**

1957, **Tempera auf Hartfaser** / Tempera on hardboard, 30 × 30 cm, 2014

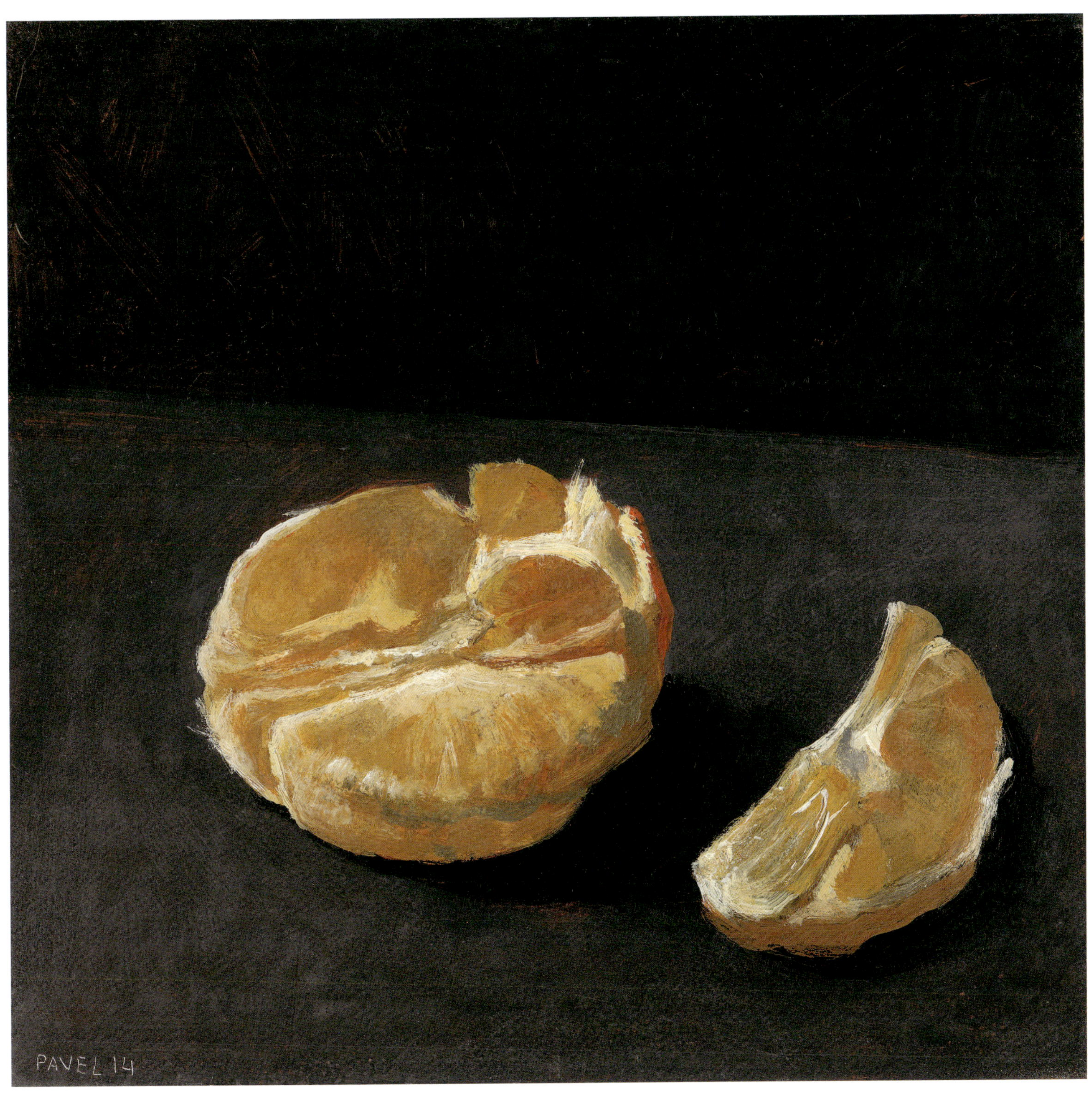
PAVEL 14

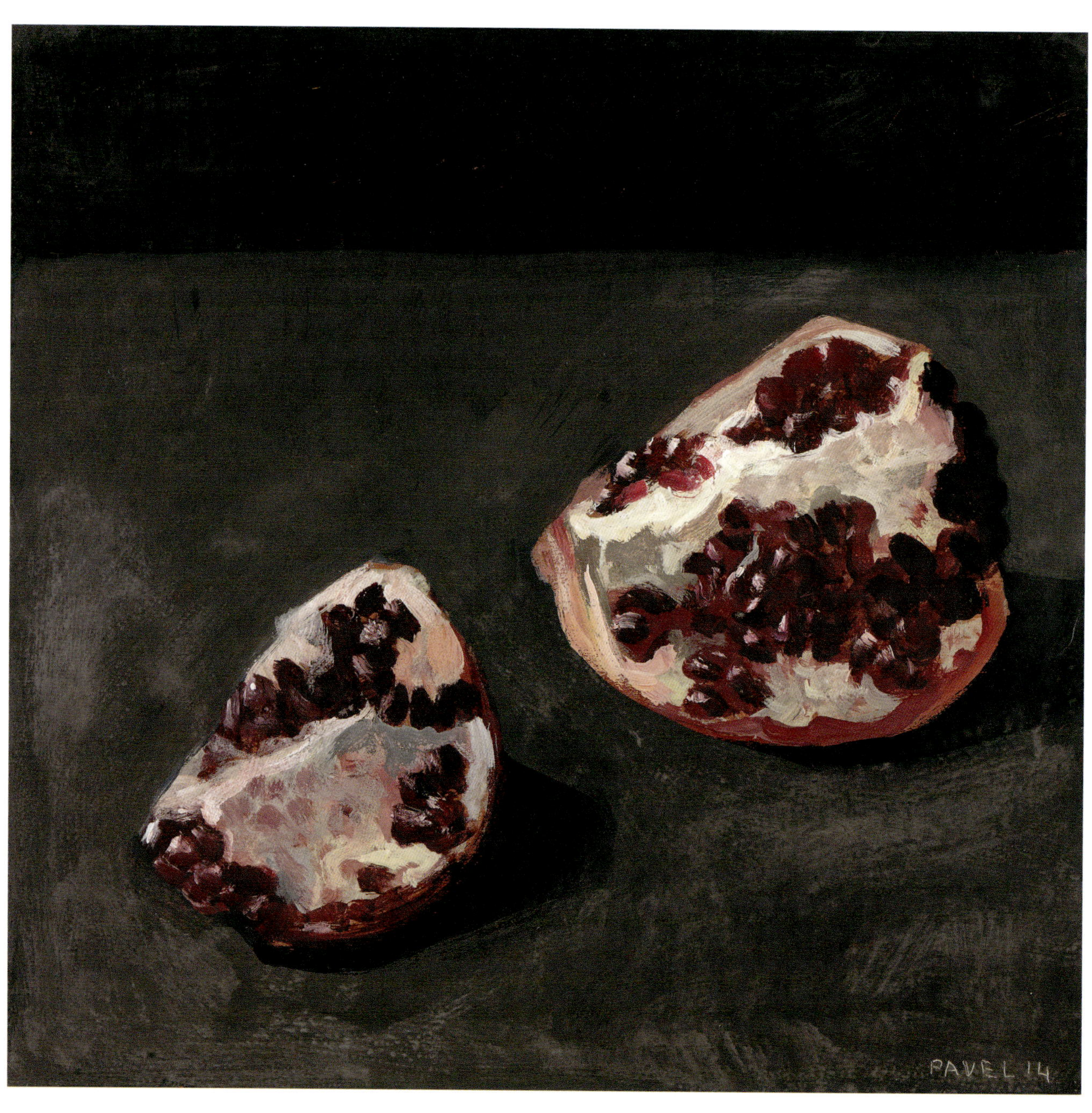

1964, **Tempera auf Hartfaser** / Tempera on hardboard, 30 × 30 cm, 2014

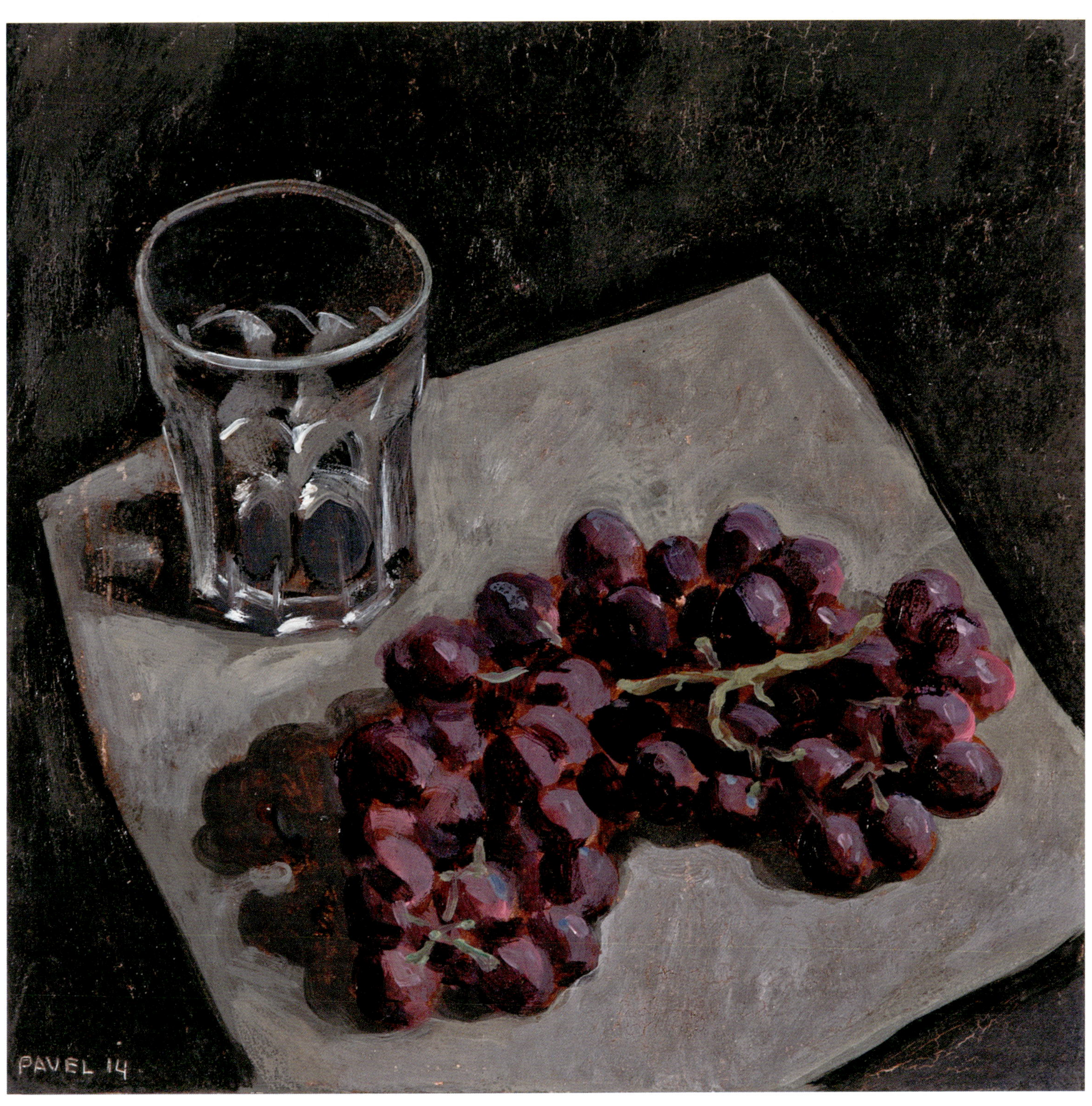

1867, **Tempera auf Hartfaser** / Tempera on hardboard, **30 × 30 cm, 2014**

1894, **Tempera auf Hartfaser** / Tempera on hardboard, 30 × 30 cm, 2014

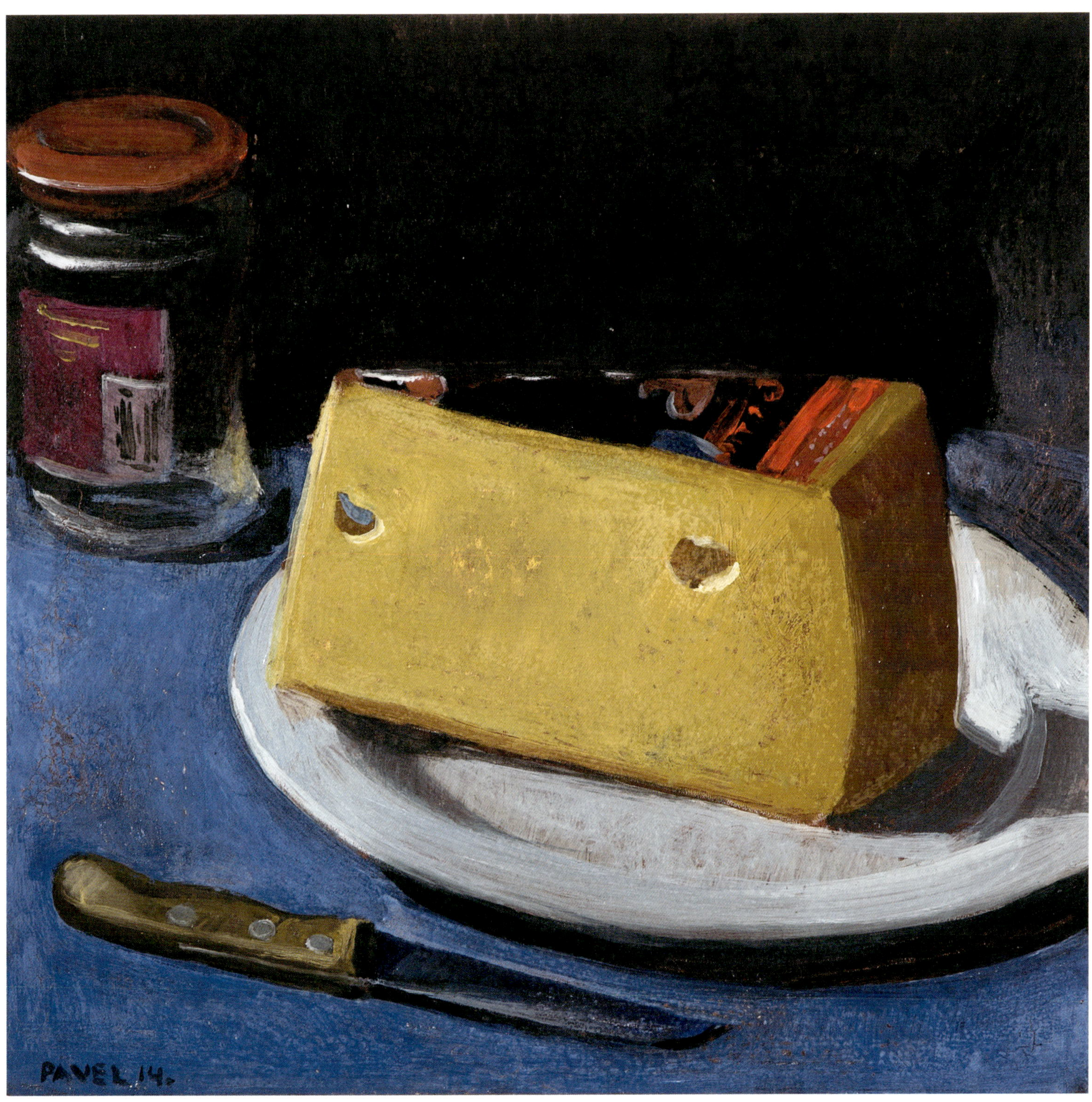
PAVEL 14.

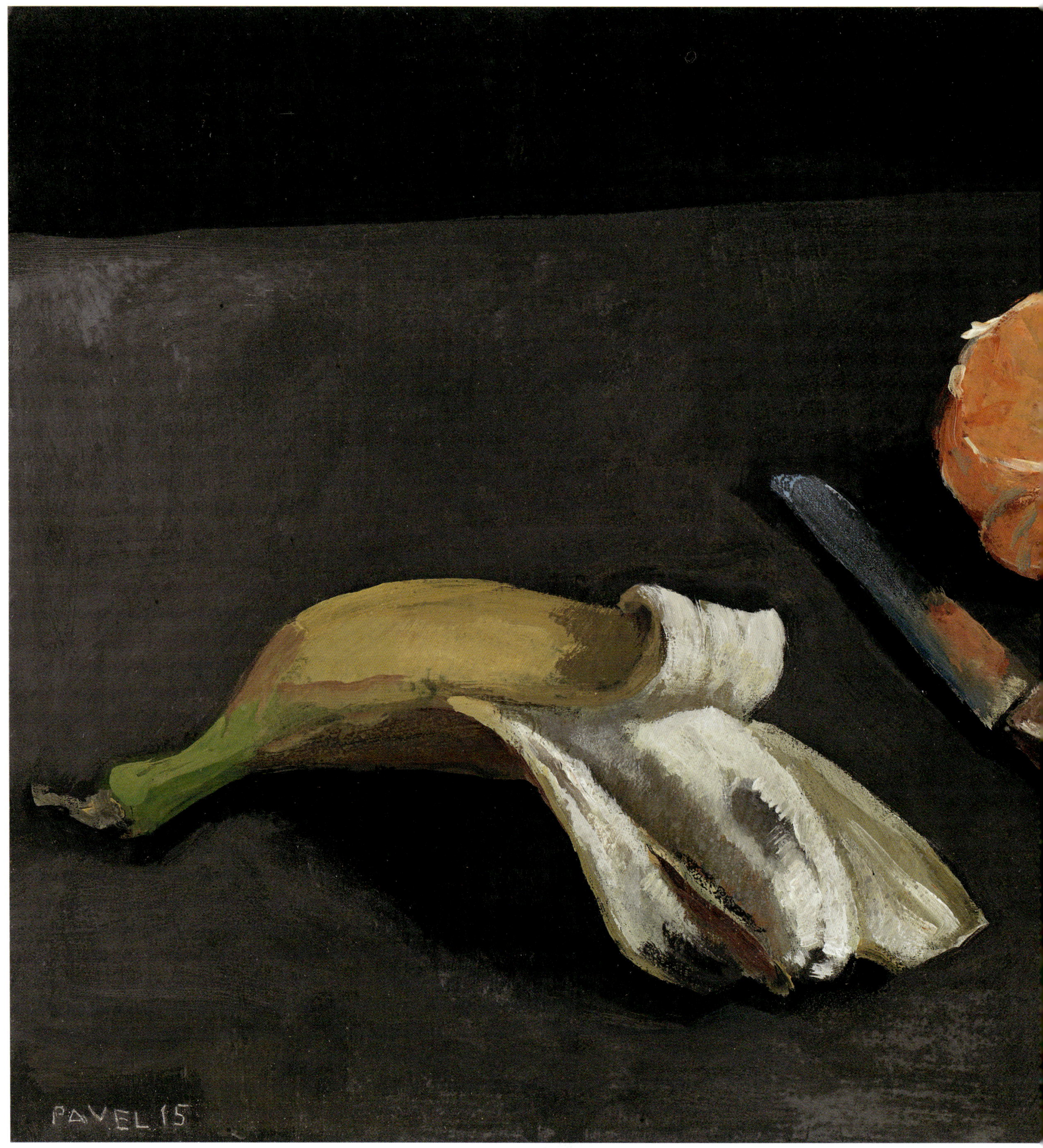
PAVEL 15

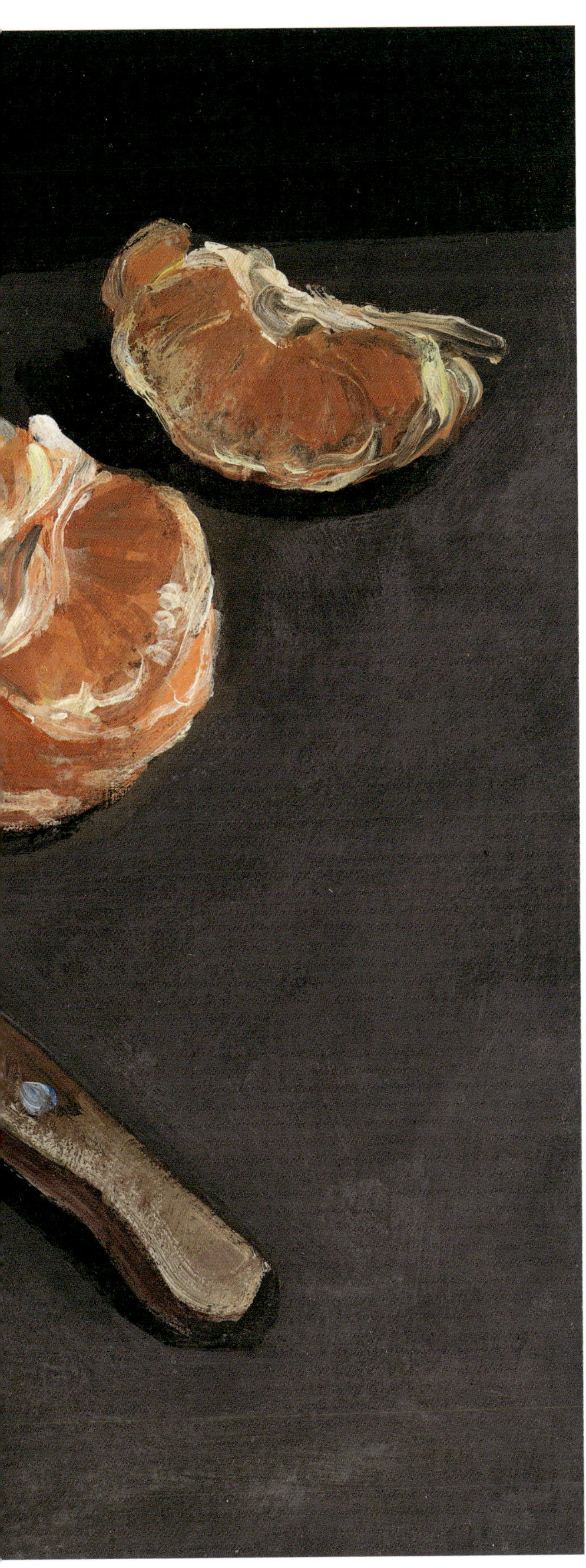

1975, **Tempera auf Hartfaser** / Tempera on hardboard, 30 × 40 cm, 2015

1841, **Tempera auf Hartfaser** / Tempera on hardboard, 30 × 30 cm, 2014

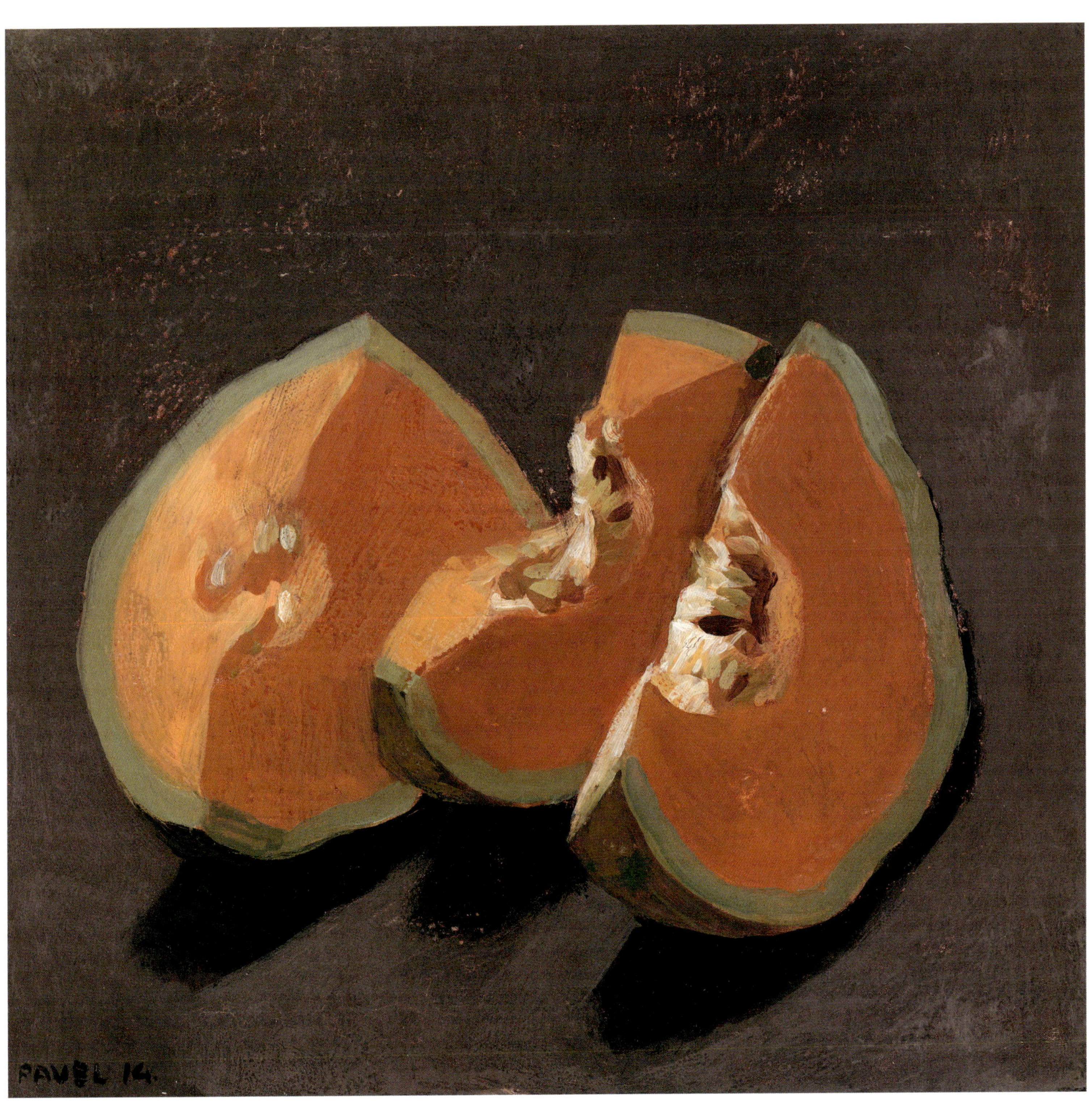
PAVEL 14.

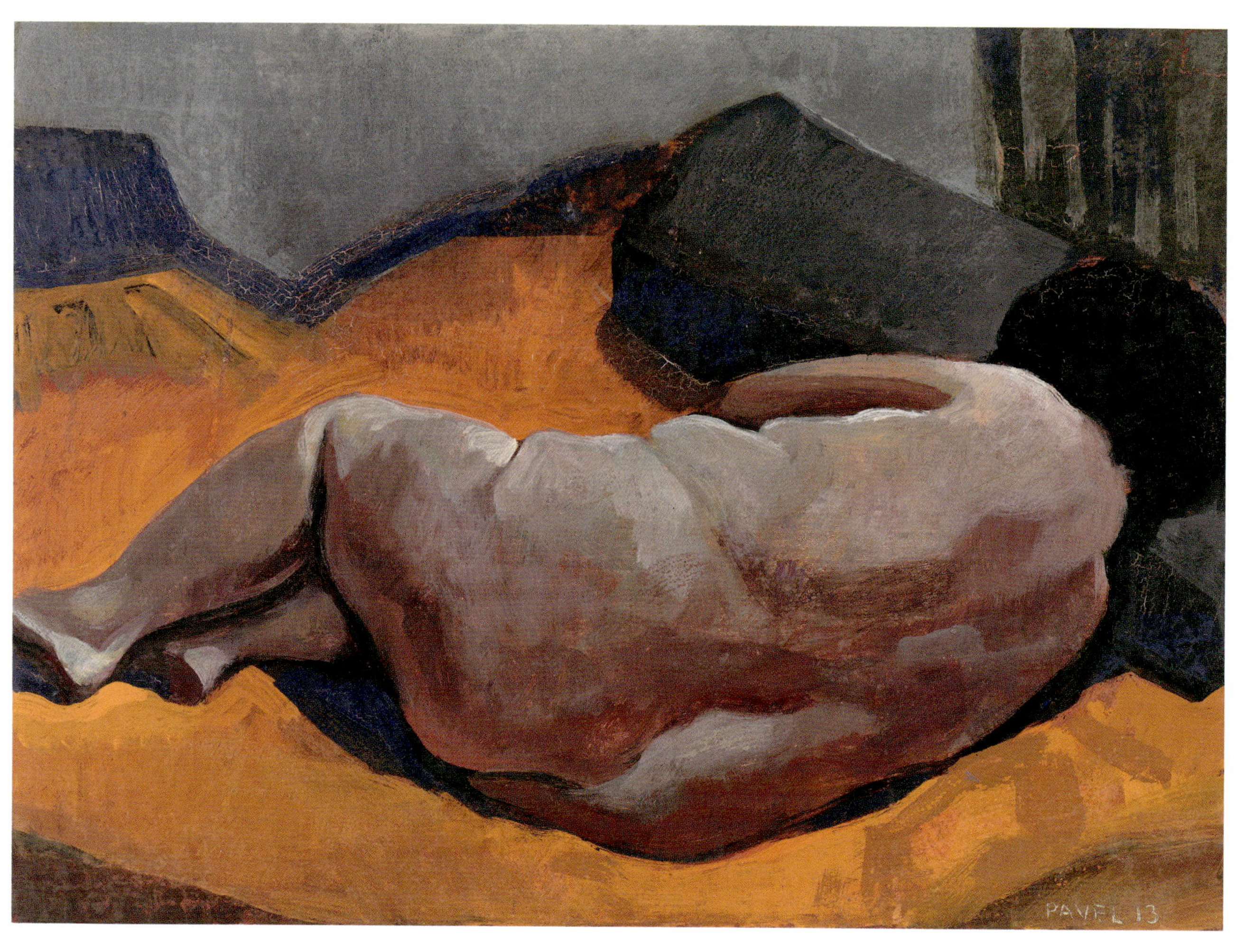

1826, **Tempera auf Hartfaser** / Tempera on hardboard, **30 × 40 cm**, 2013

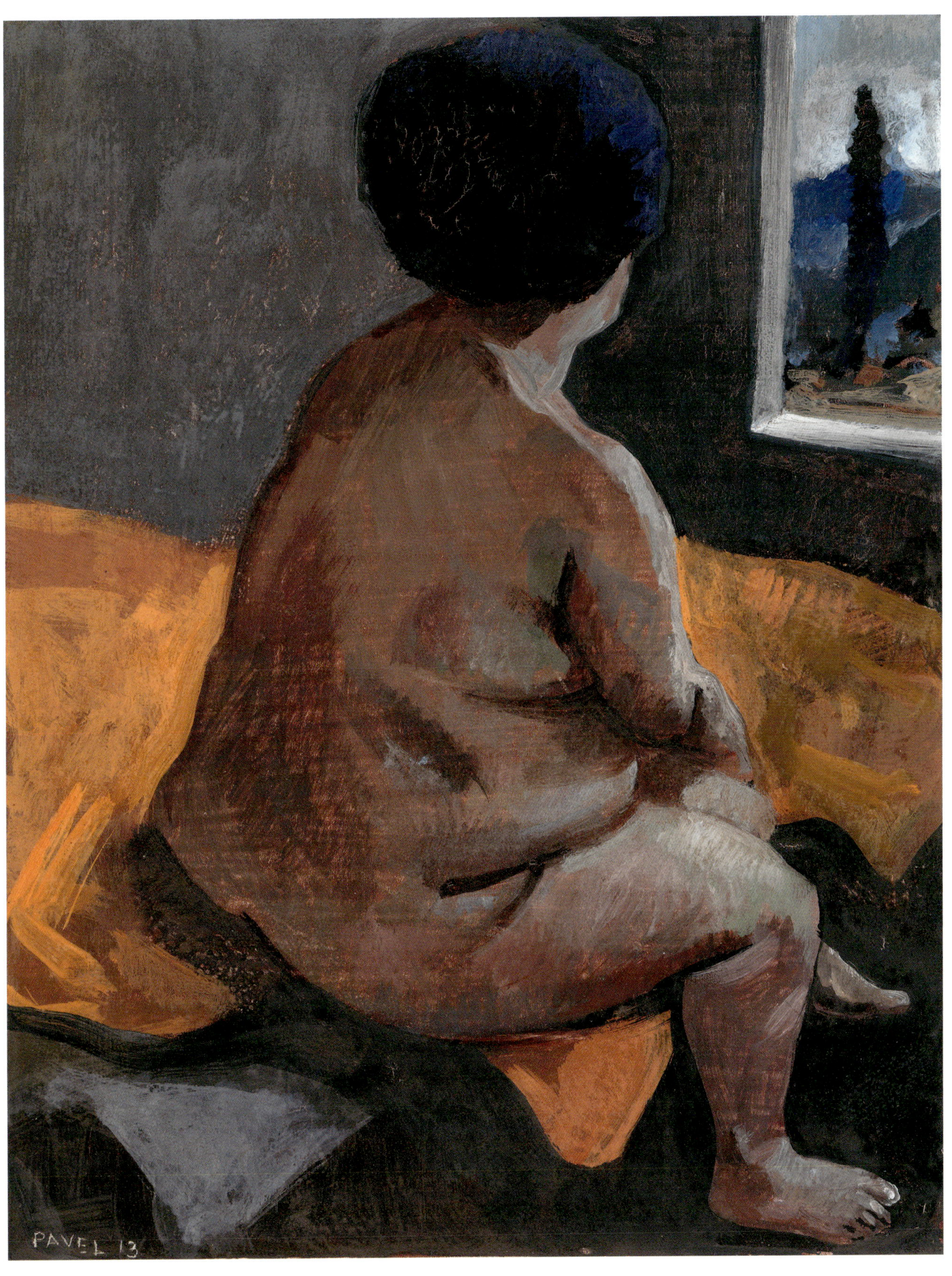

1828, **Tempera auf Hartfaser** / Tempera on hardboard, 40 × 30 cm, 2013

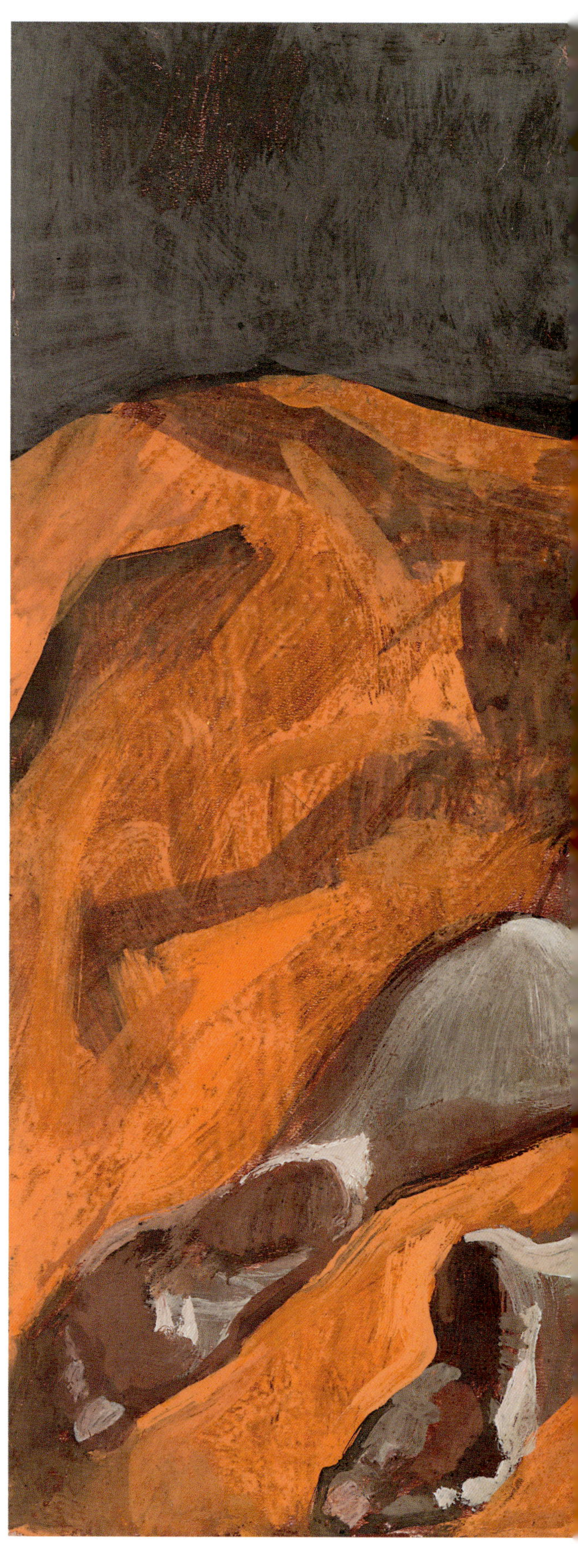

1827, **Tempera auf Hartfaser** / Tempera on hardboard, **30 × 40 cm**, 2013

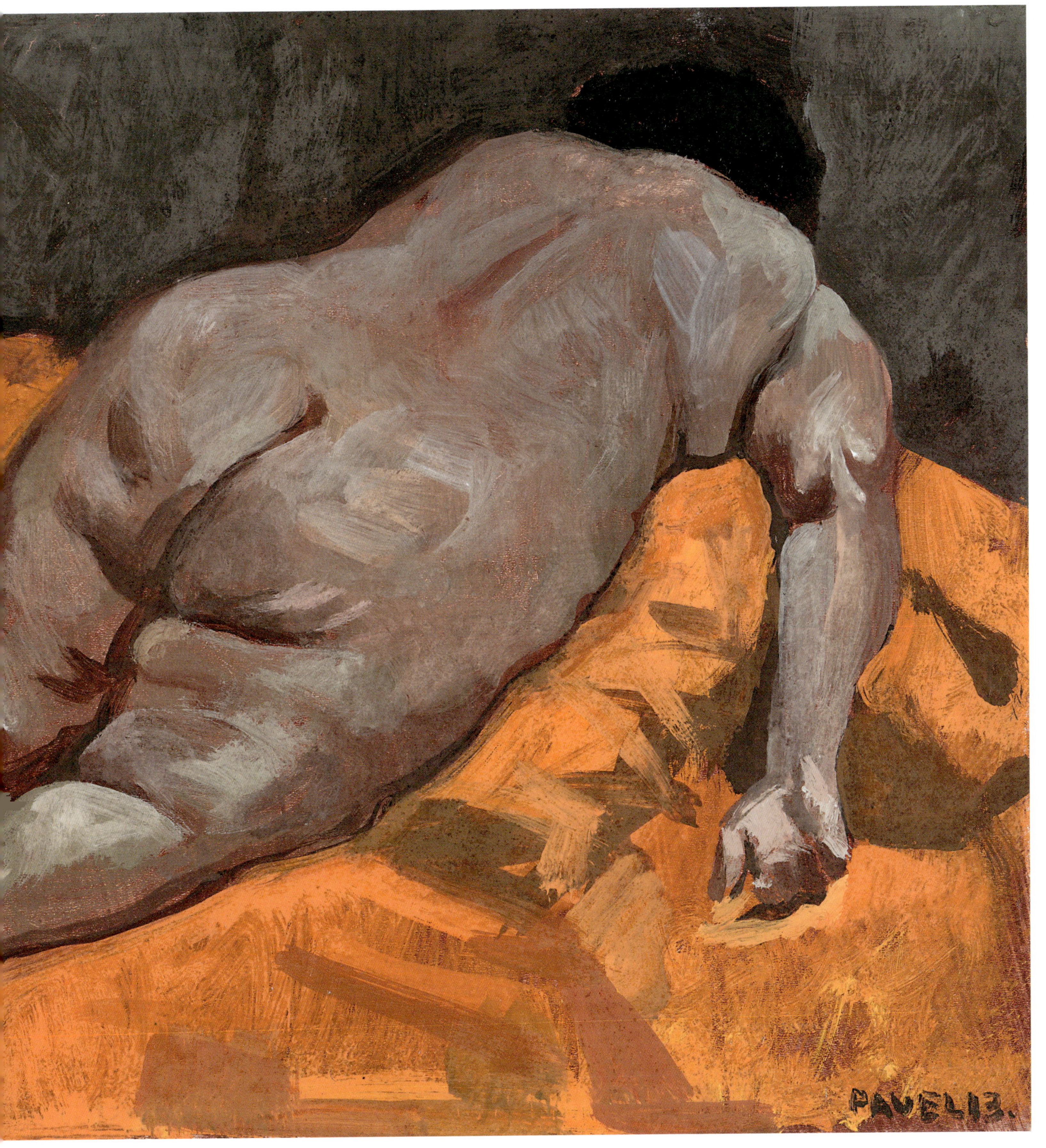
PAVELIĆ.

1850, **Tempera auf Hartfaser** / Tempera on hardboard, 30 × 30 cm, 2014

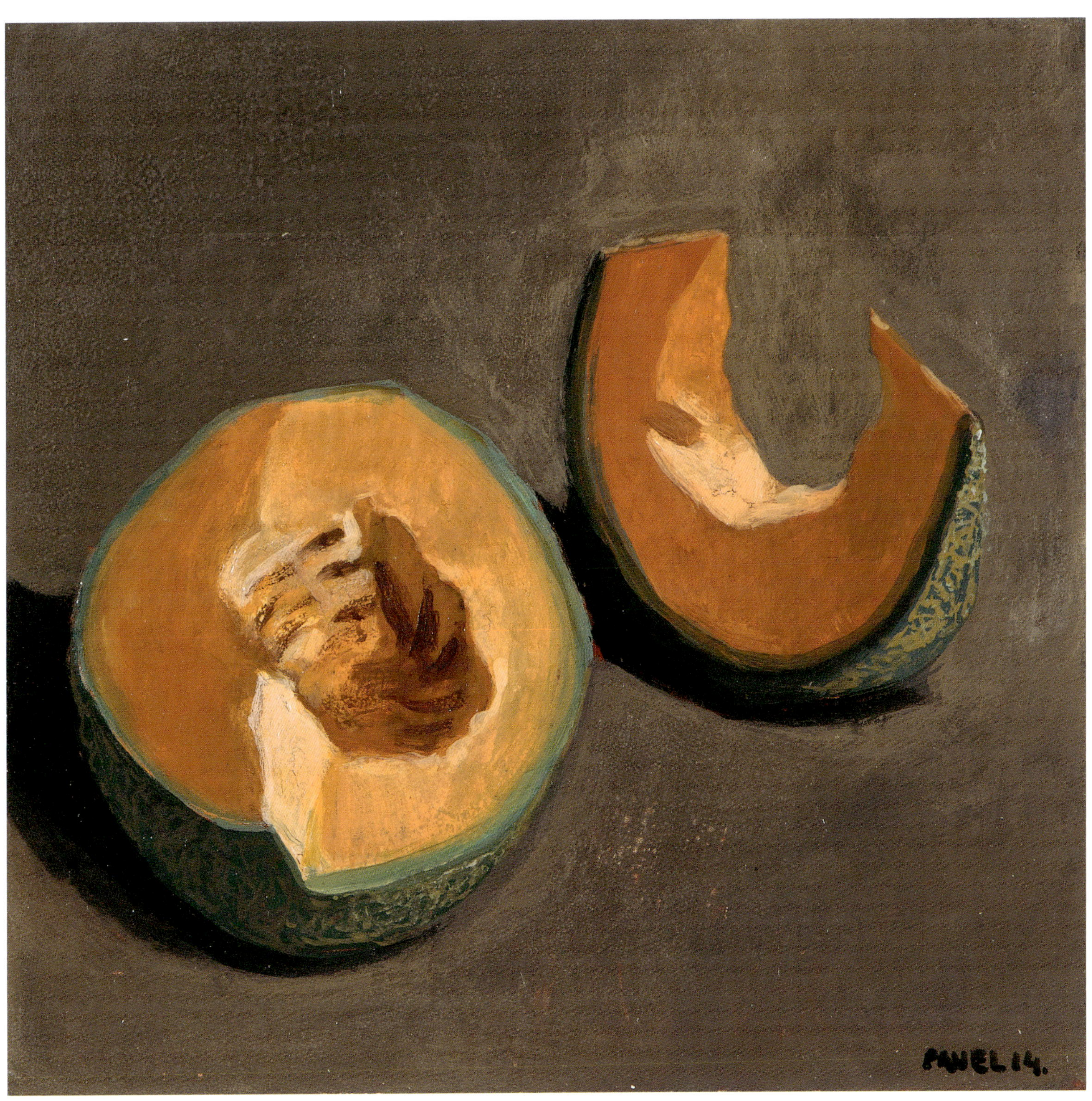

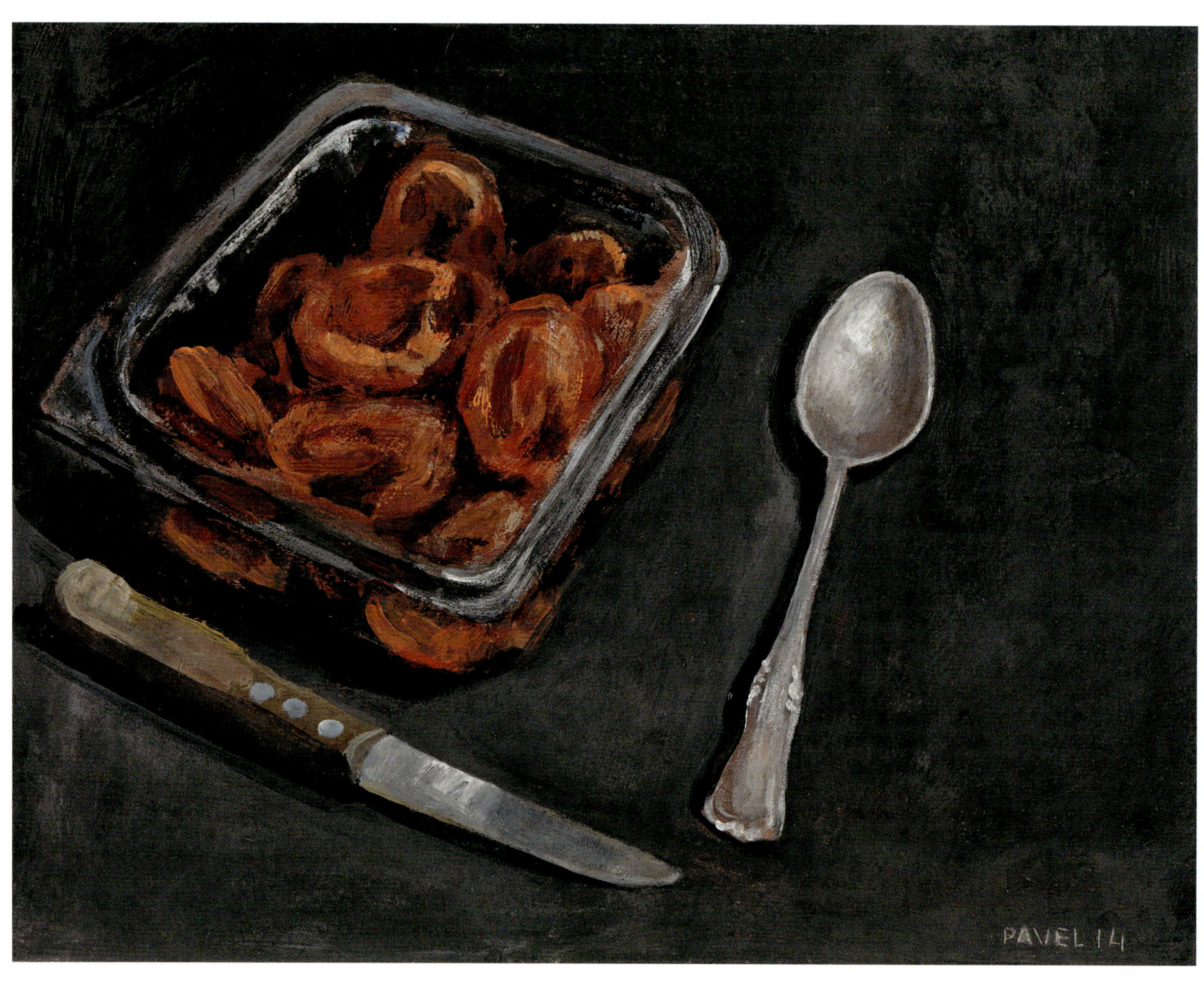

1968, **Tempera auf Hartfaser** / Tempera on hardboard, 24 × 30 cm, 2014

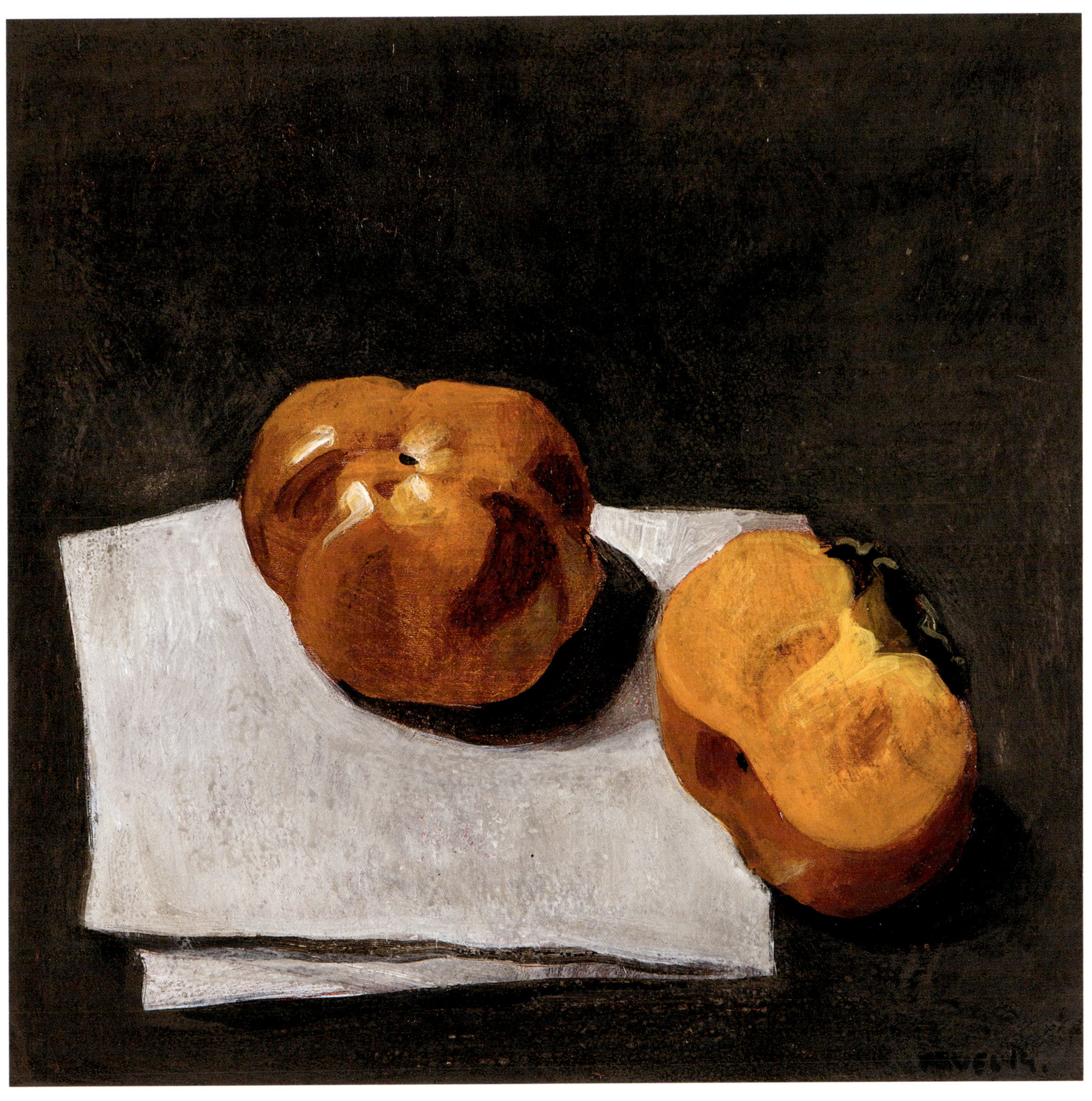

1842, **Tempera auf Hartfaser** / Tempera on hardboard, 30 × 30 cm, 2014

1934, **Tempera auf Hartfaser** / Tempera on hardboard, 30 × 40 cm, 2014

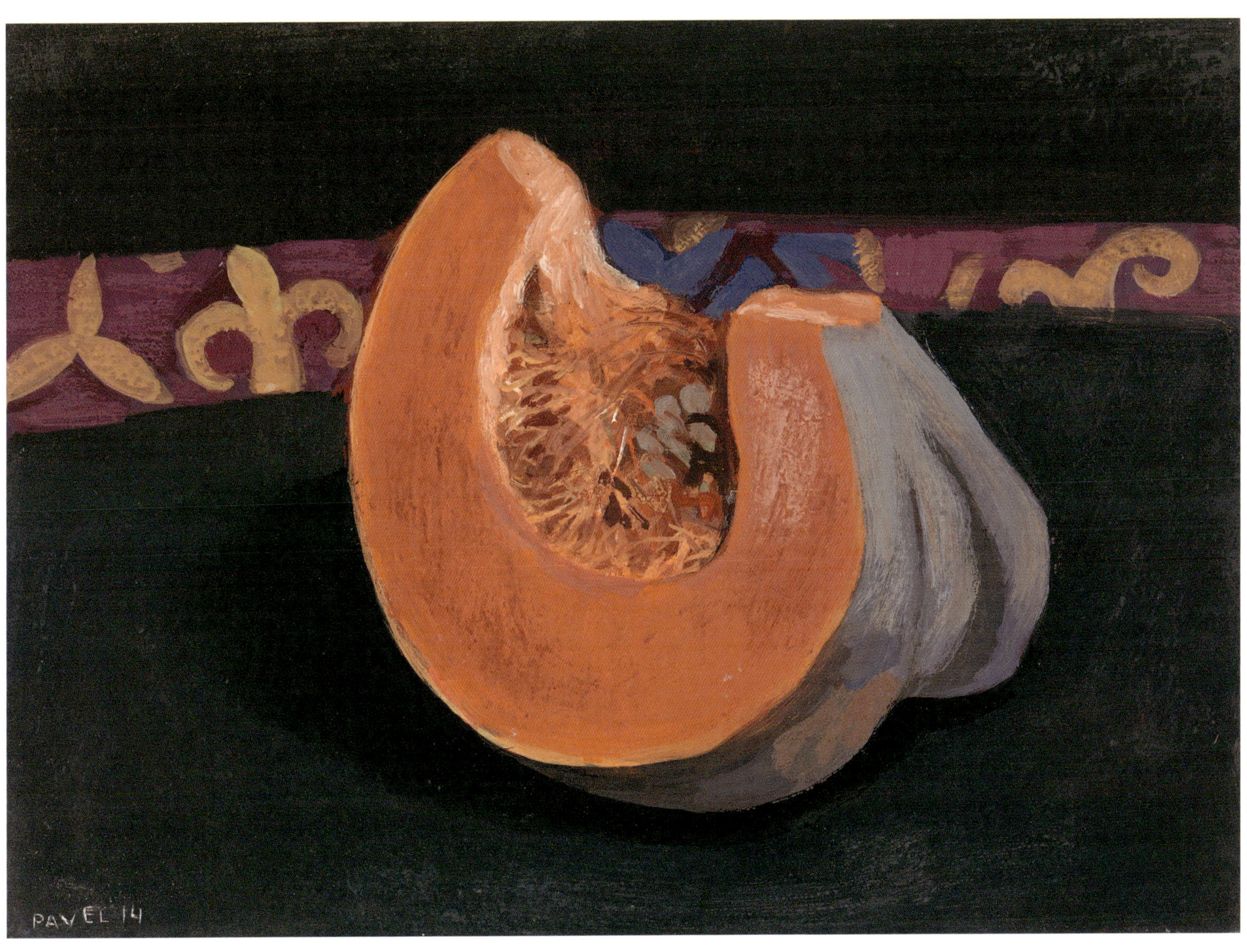
PAVEL 14

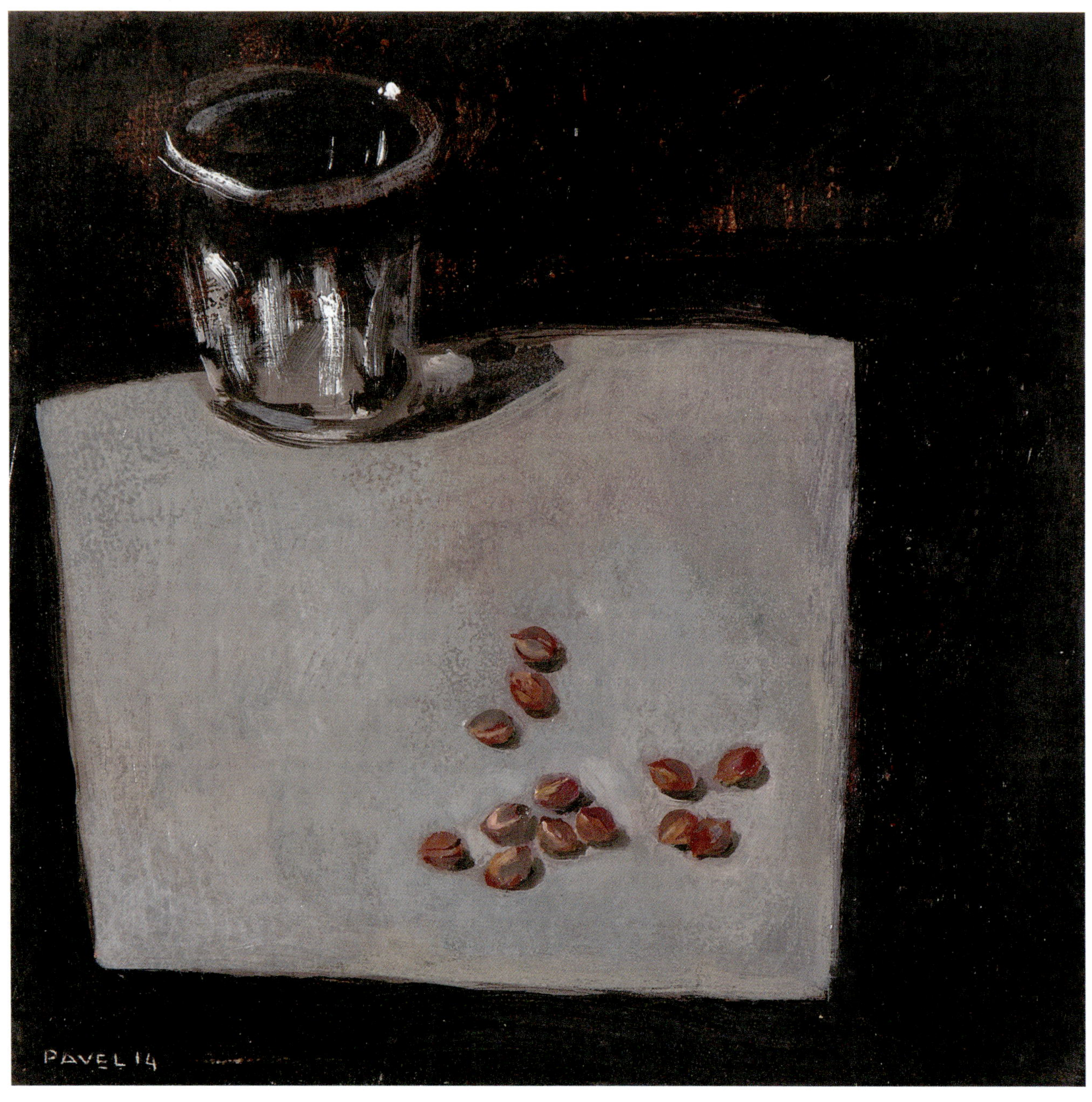

1883, **Tempera auf Hartfaser** / Tempera on hardboard, **30 × 30 cm, 2014**

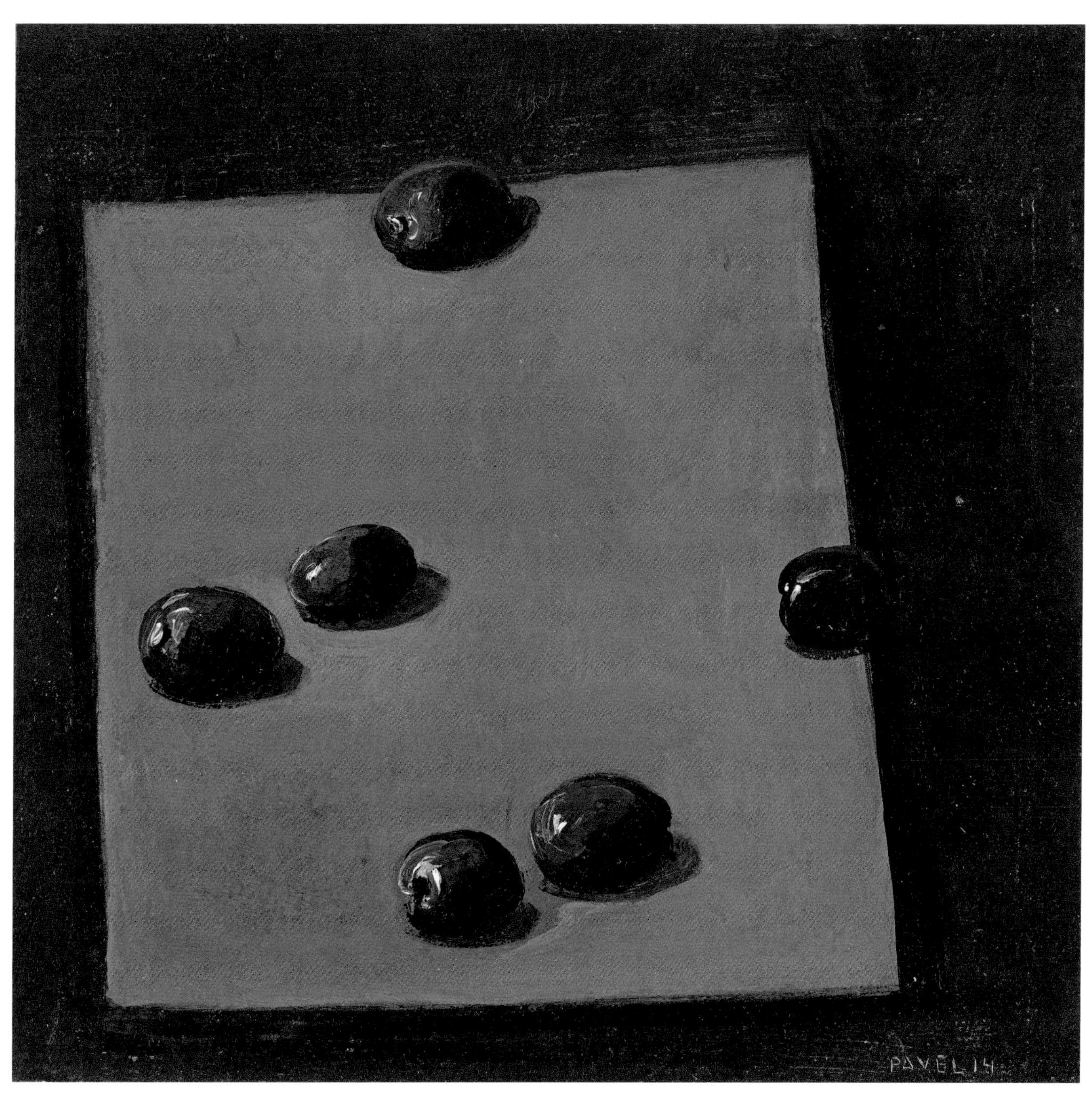

1859, **Tempera auf Hartfaser** / Tempera on hardboard, 30 × 30 **cm**, 2014

1732, **Tempera auf Hartfaser** / Tempera on hardboard, **40 × 30 cm, 2013**

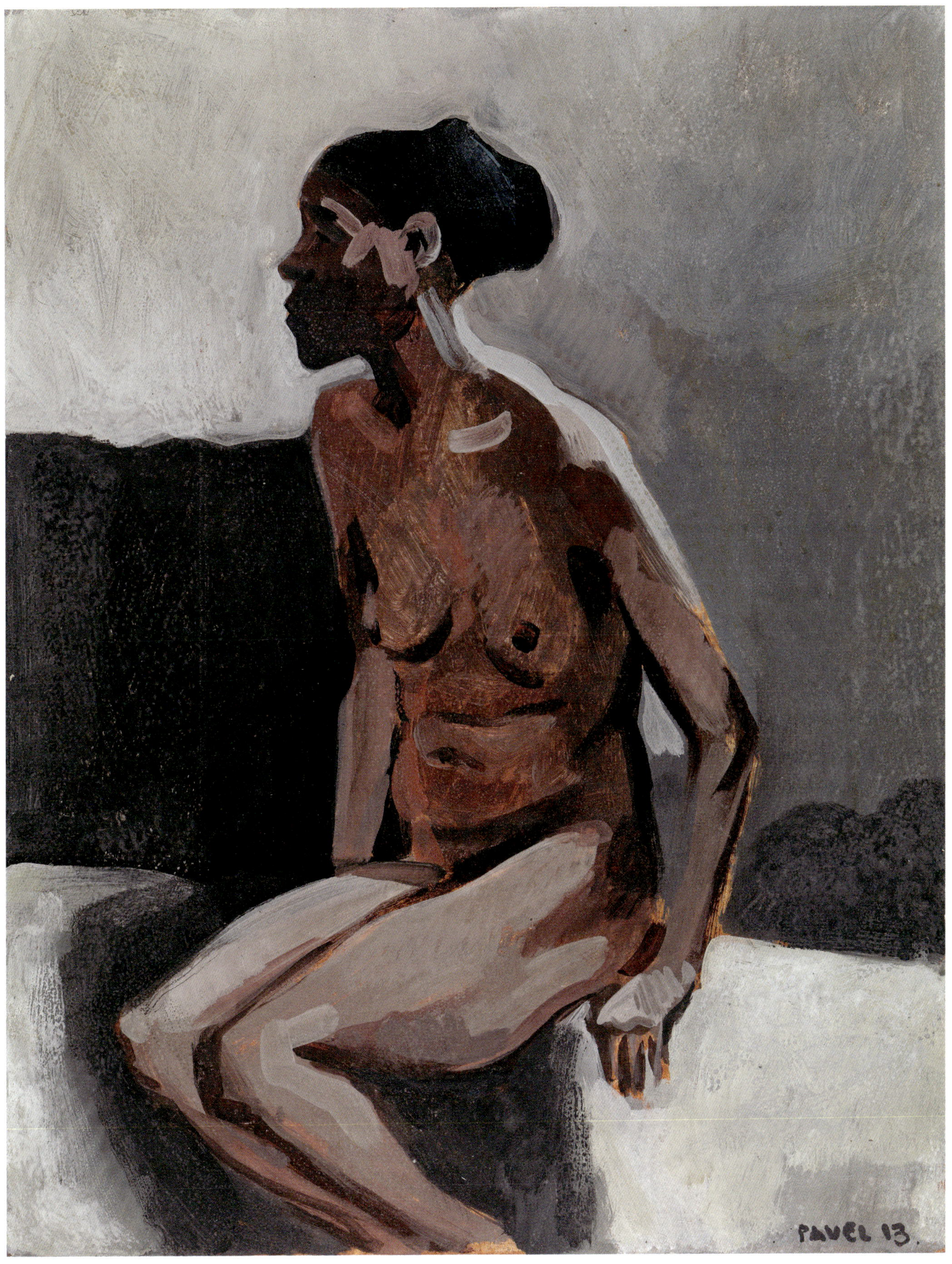
PAVEL 13.

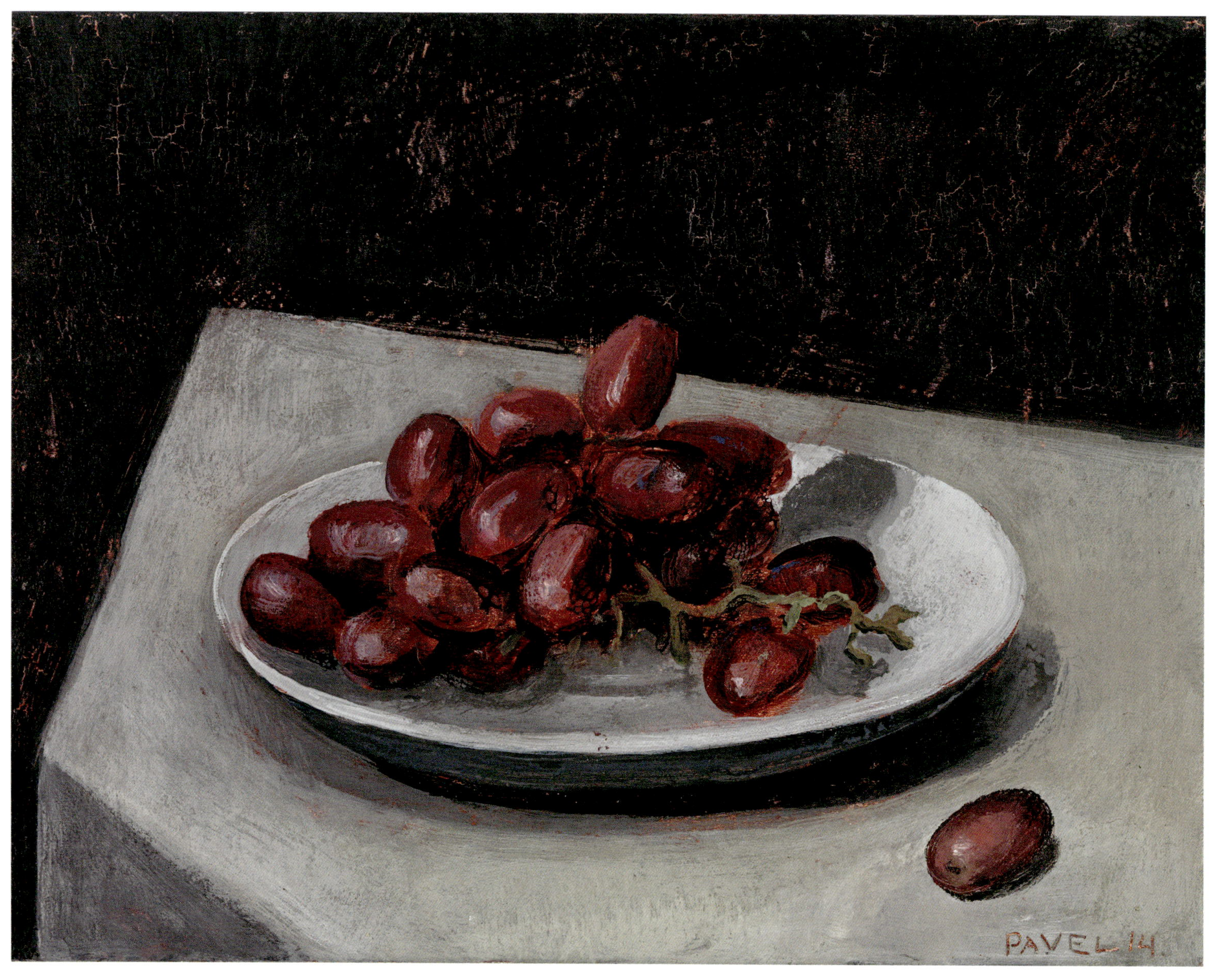

1858, **Tempera auf Hartfaser** / Tempera on hardboard, **24 × 30 cm, 2014**

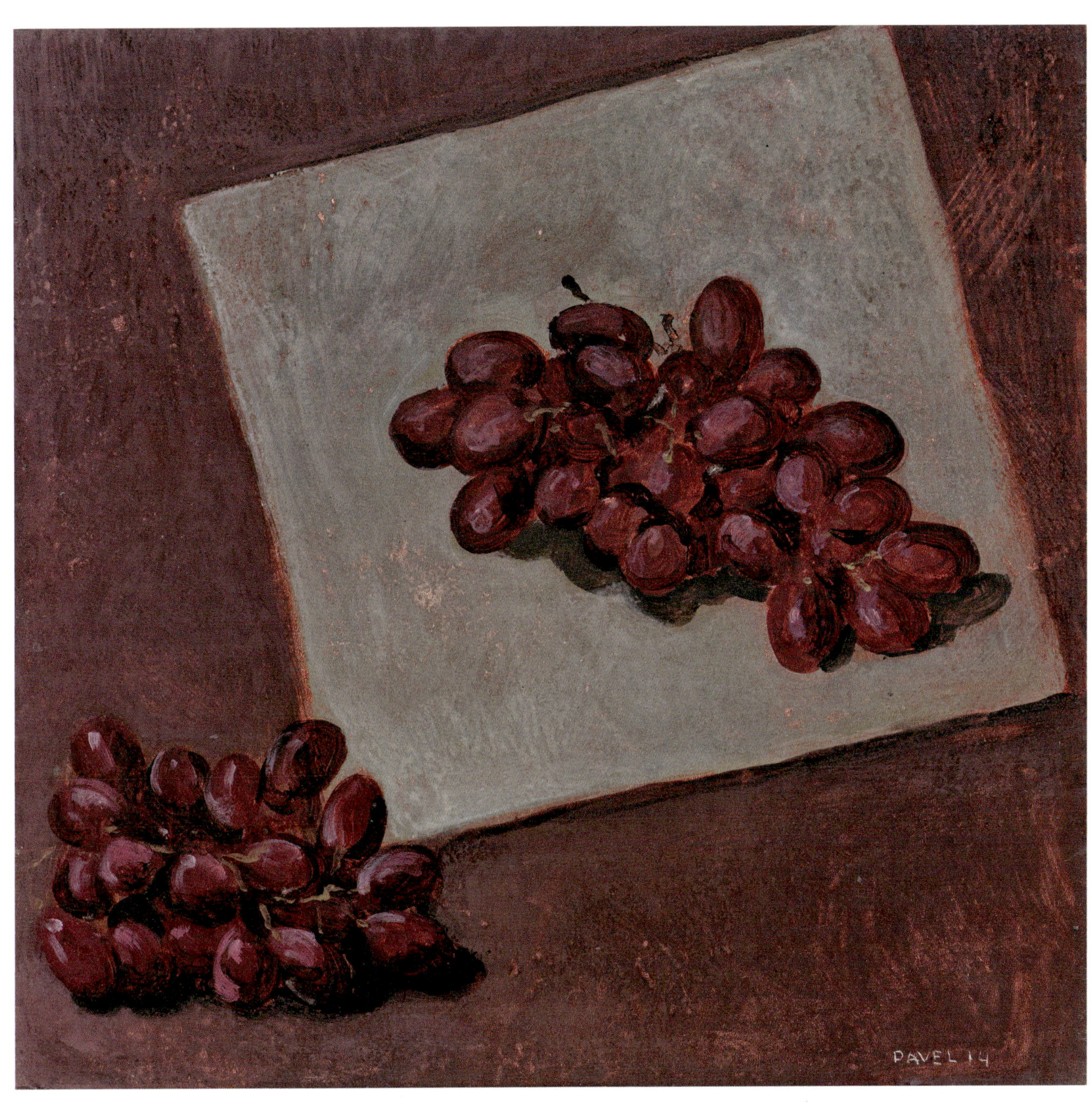

1861, **Tempera auf Hartfaser** / Tempera on hardboard, 30 × 30 cm, 2014

1928, **Tempera auf Hartfaser** / Tempera on hardboard, 30 × 30 cm, 2014

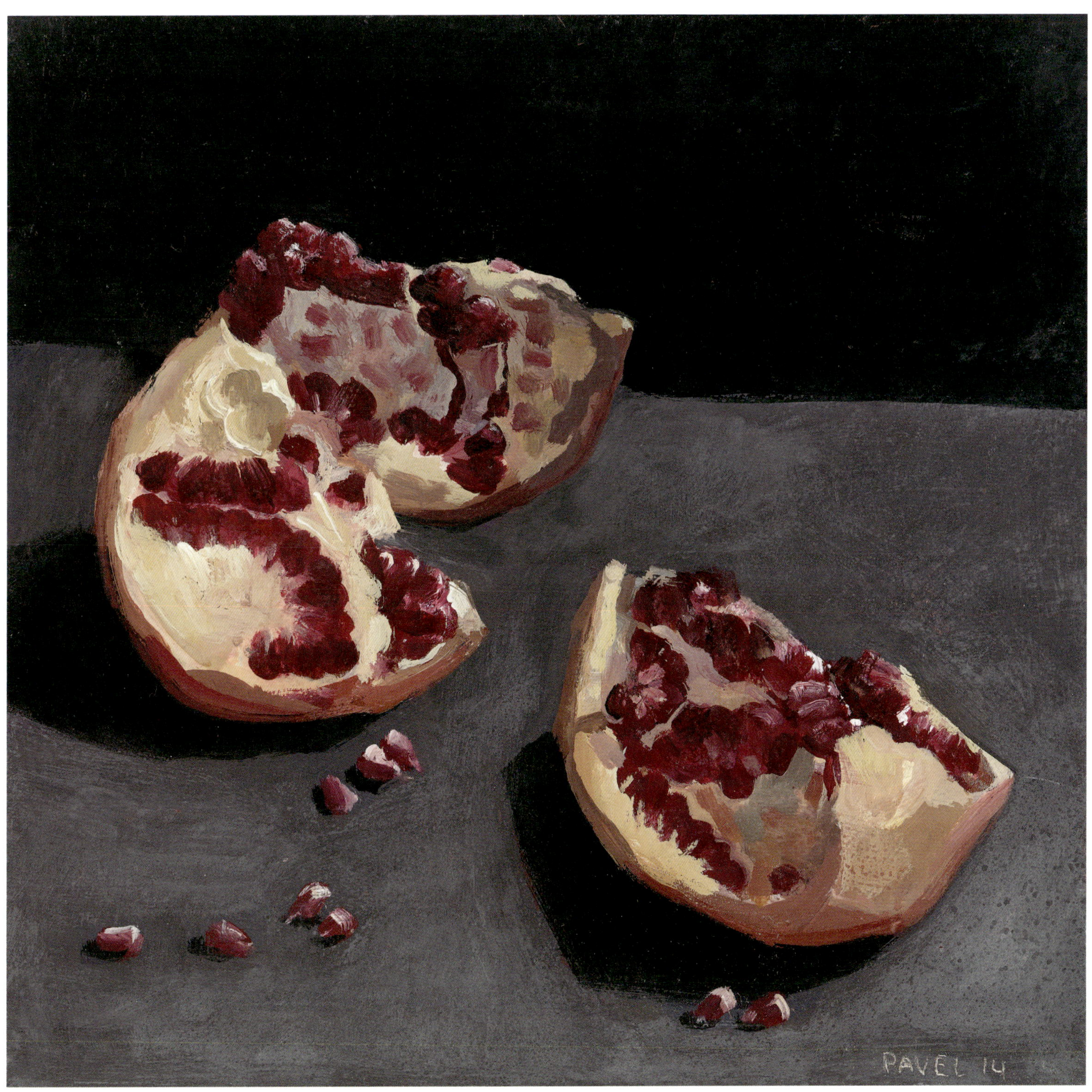
PAVEL 14

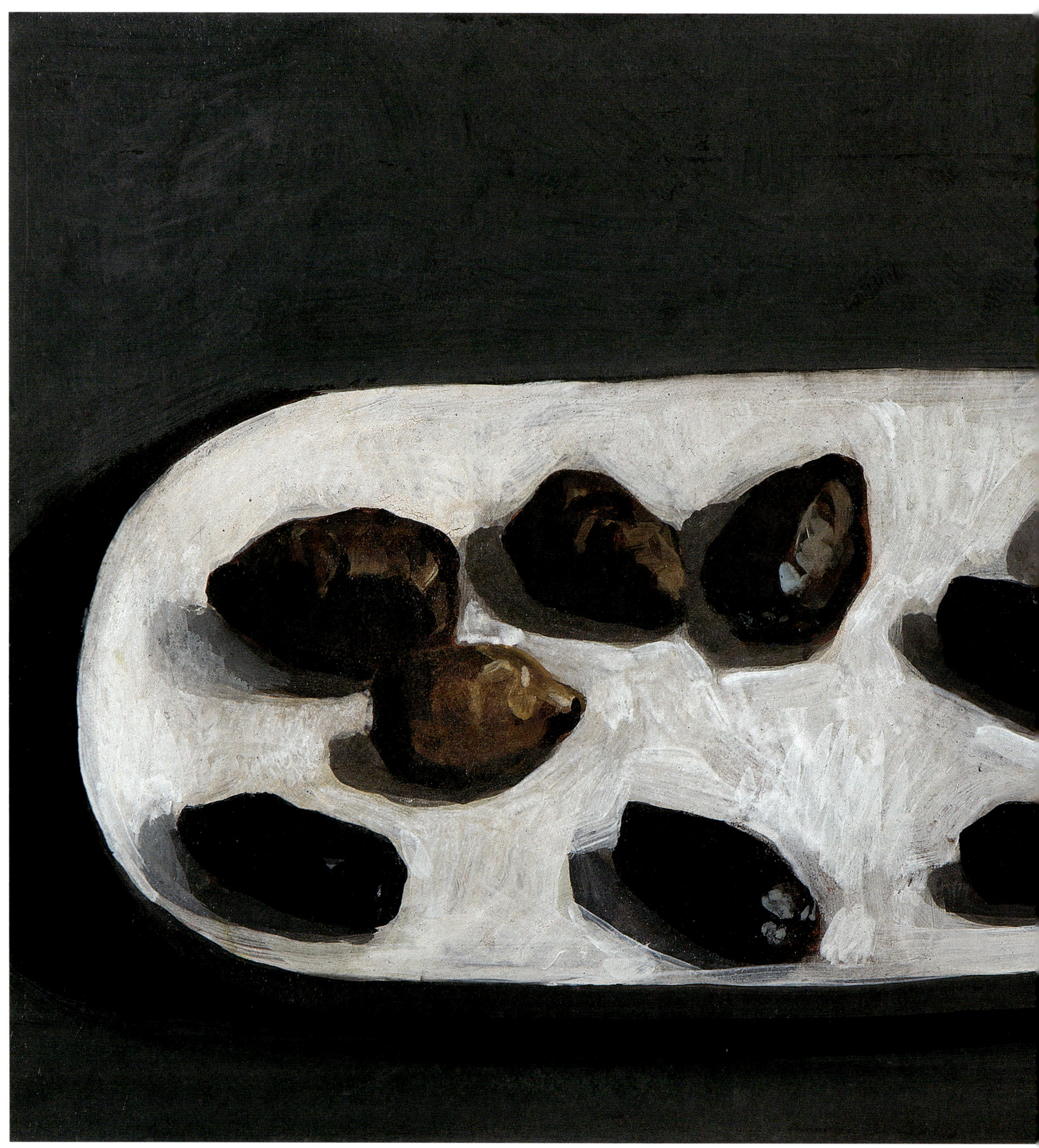

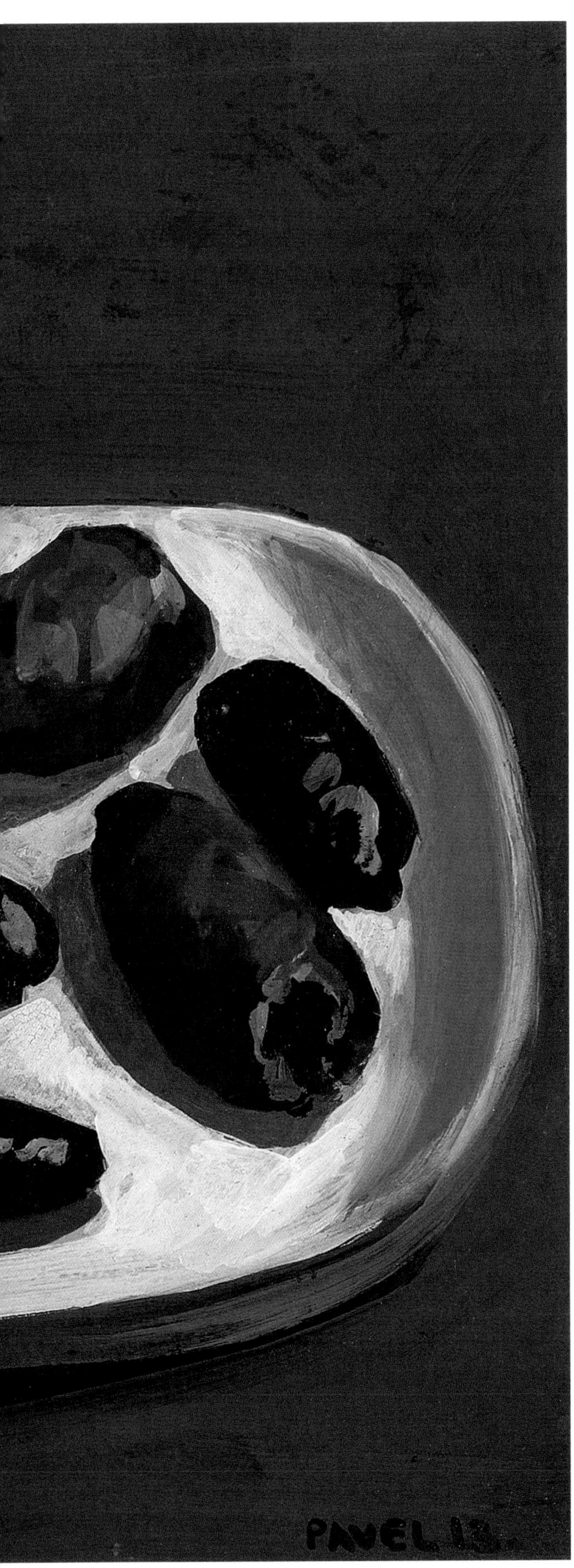

1794, **Tempera auf Hartfaser** / Tempera on hardboard, 30 × 40 cm, 2013

1956, **Tempera auf Hartfaser** / Tempera on hardboard, 30 × 30 cm, 2014

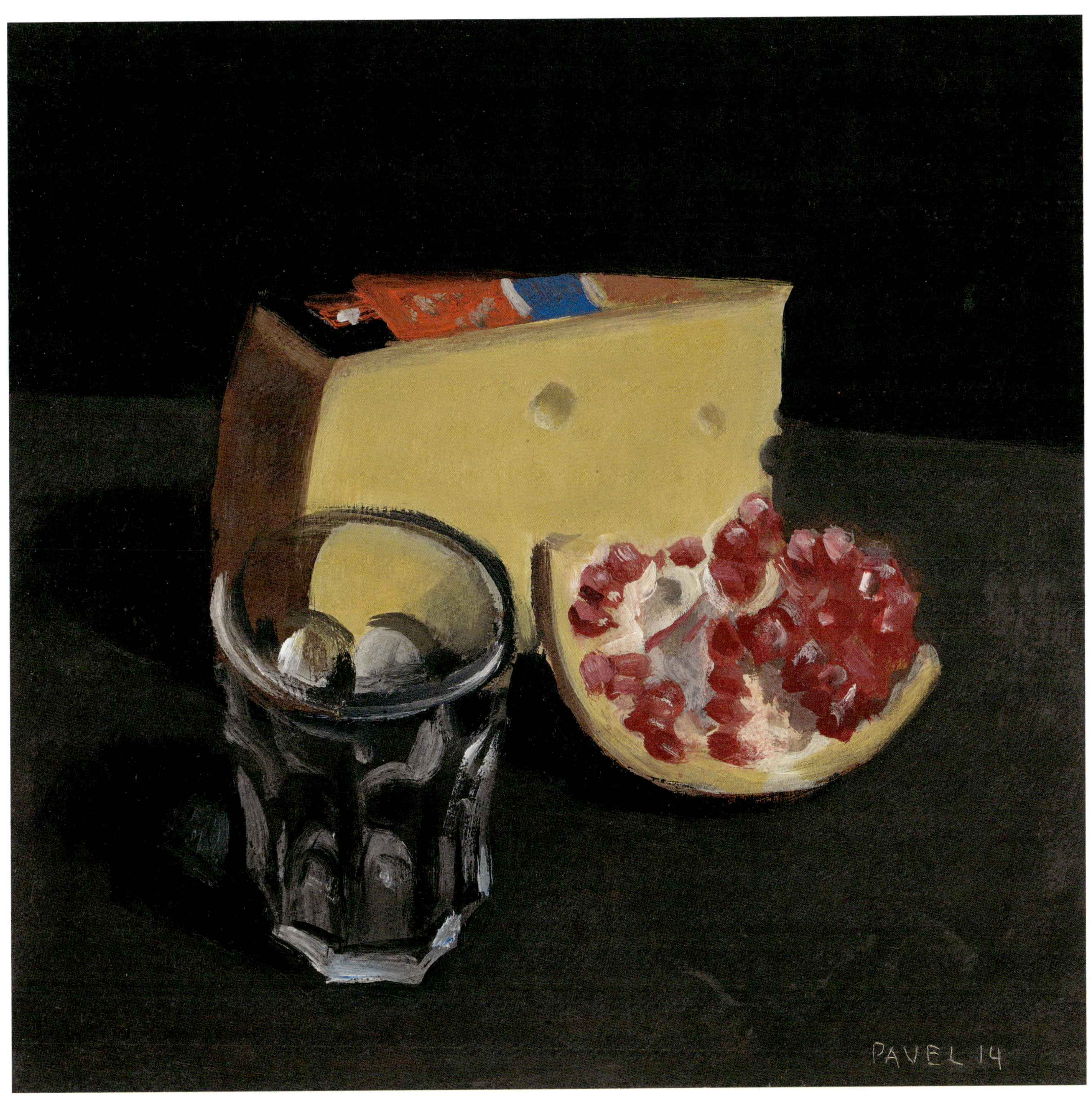
PAVEL 14

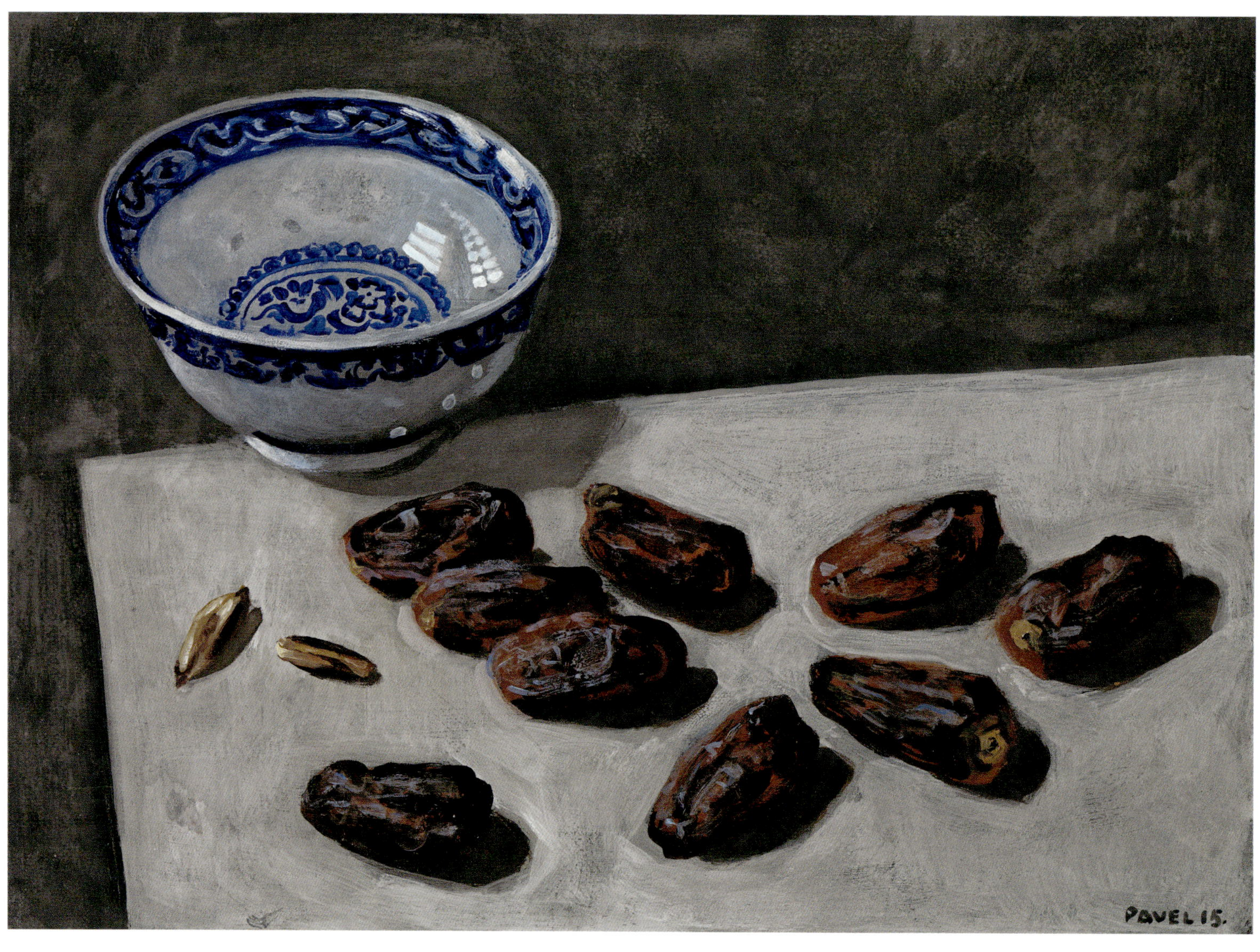

1978, **Tempera auf Hartfaser** / Tempera on hardboard, 30 × 40 cm, 2015

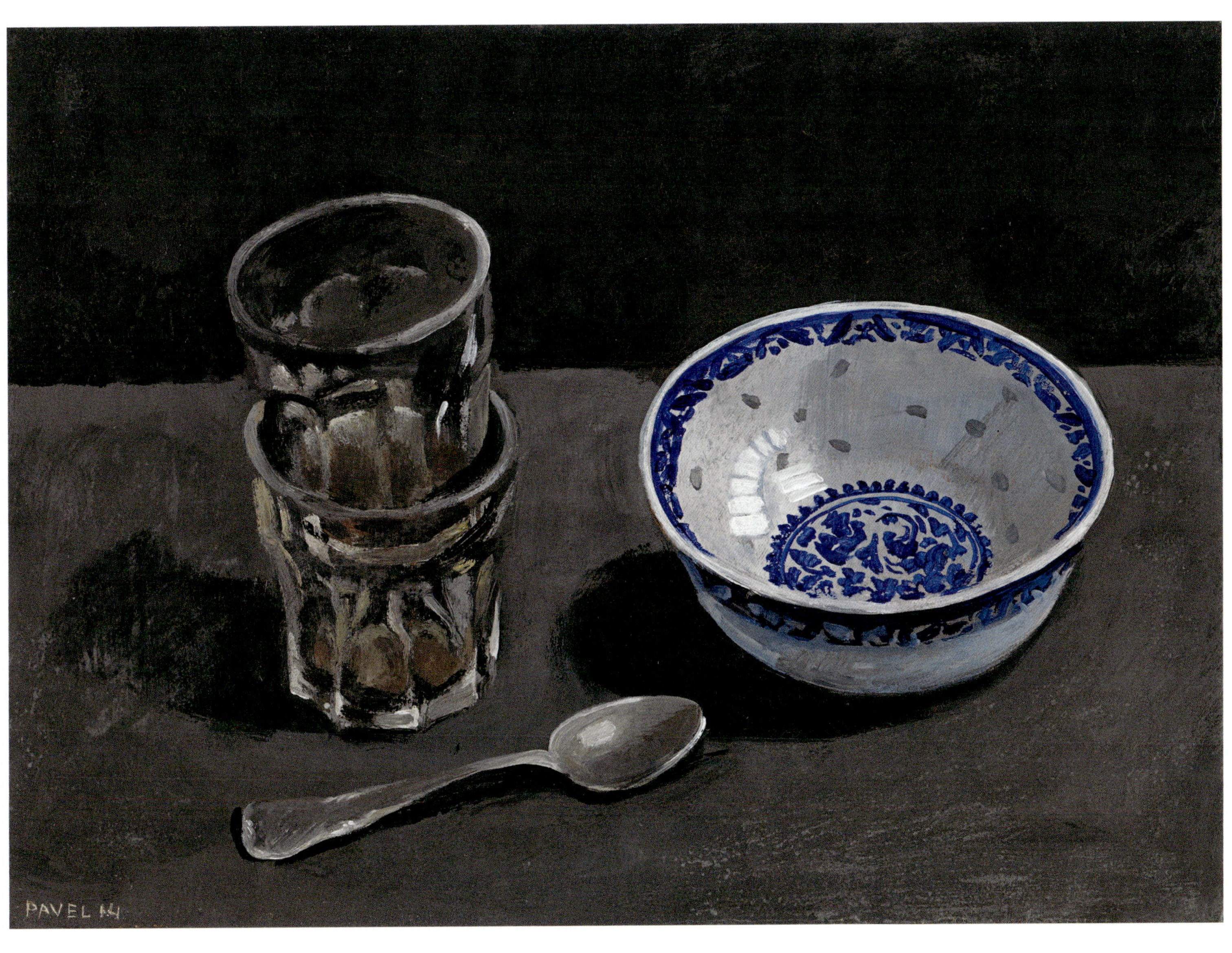

1969, **Tempera auf Hartfaser** / Tempera on hardboard, **30 × 40 cm, 2014**

1970, **Tempera auf Hartfaser** / Tempera on hardboard, **30 × 40 cm, 2014**

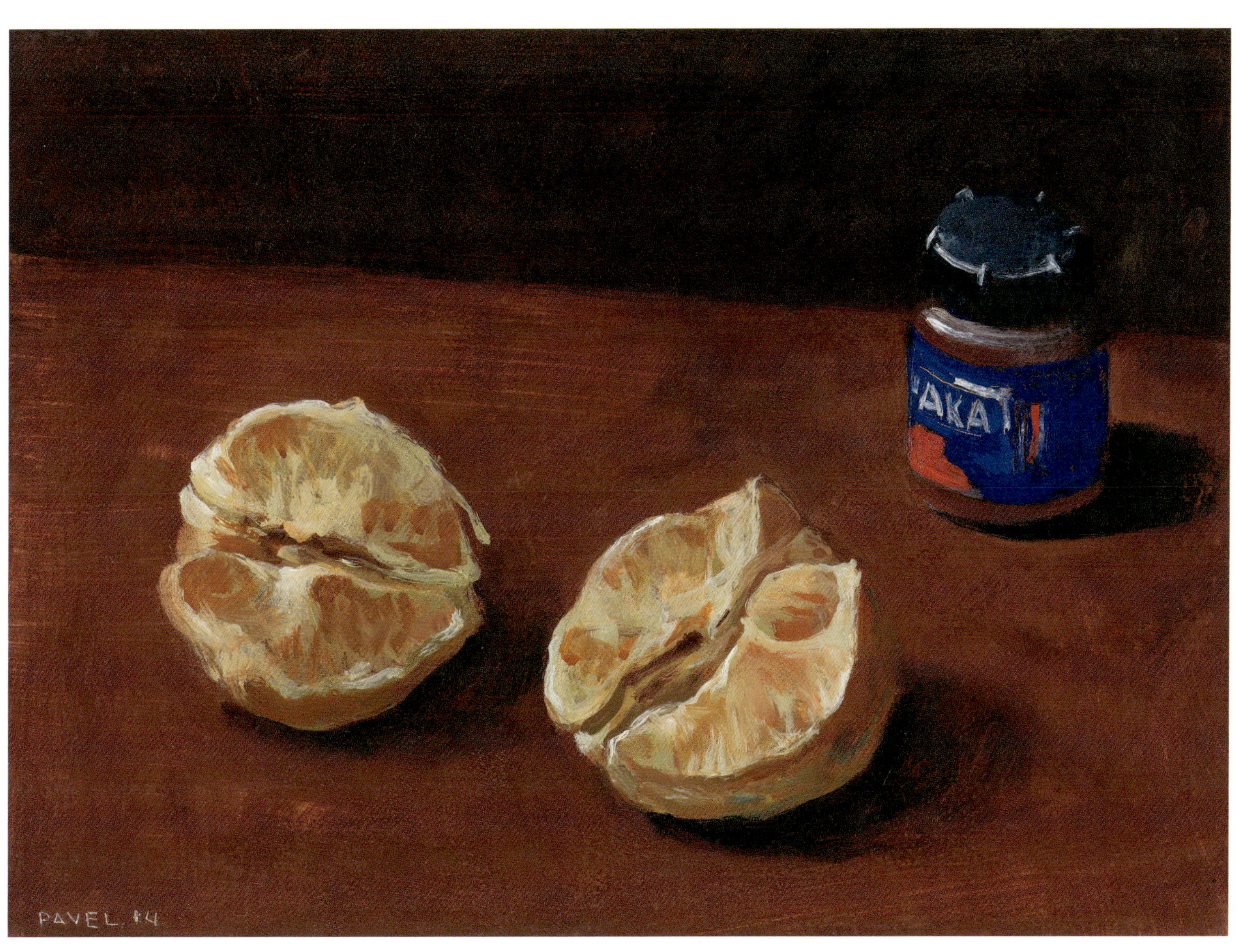
AKA
PAVEL. 84

1813, **Tempera auf Hartfaser** / Tempera on hardboard, 40 × 30 cm, 2013

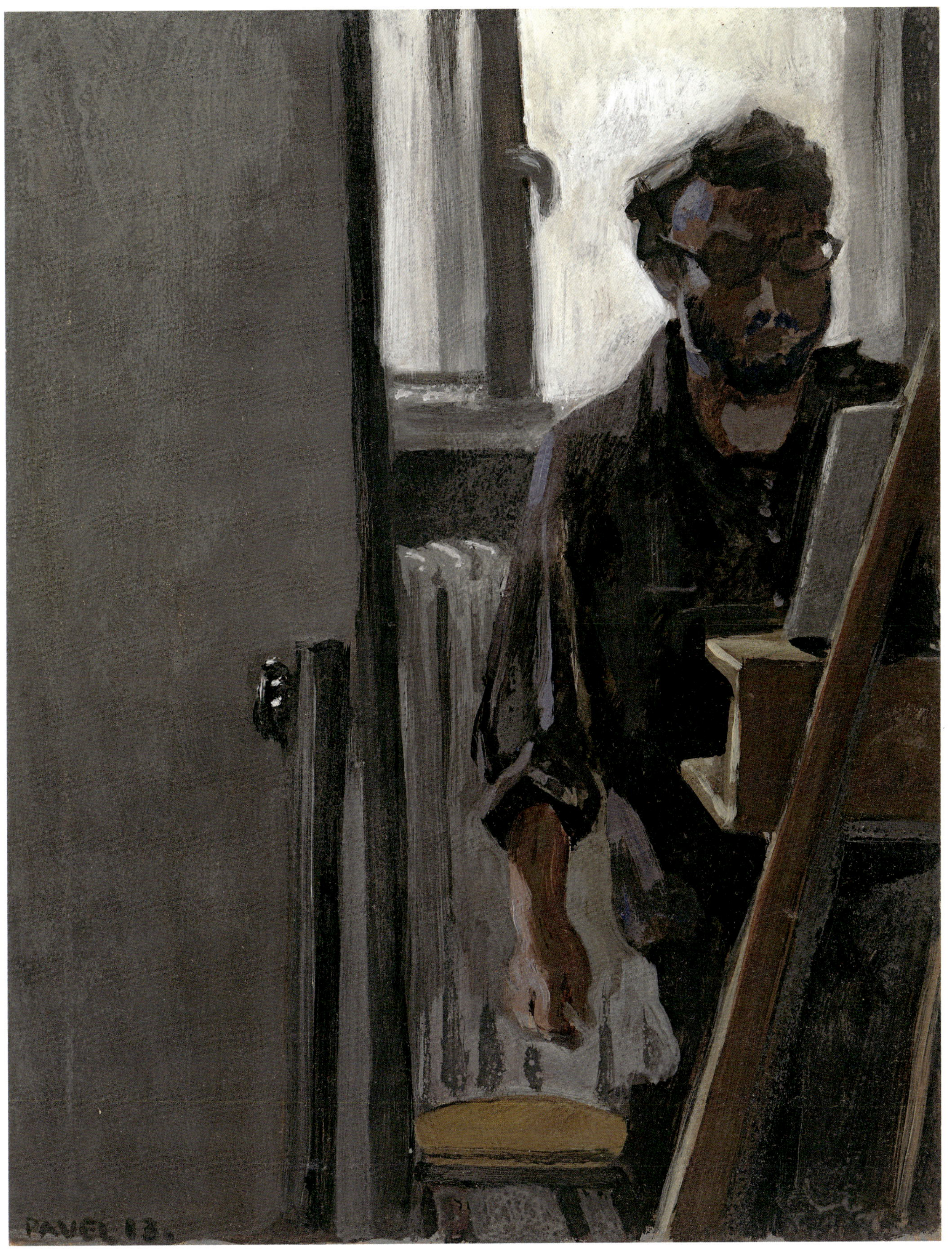
PAVEL 83.

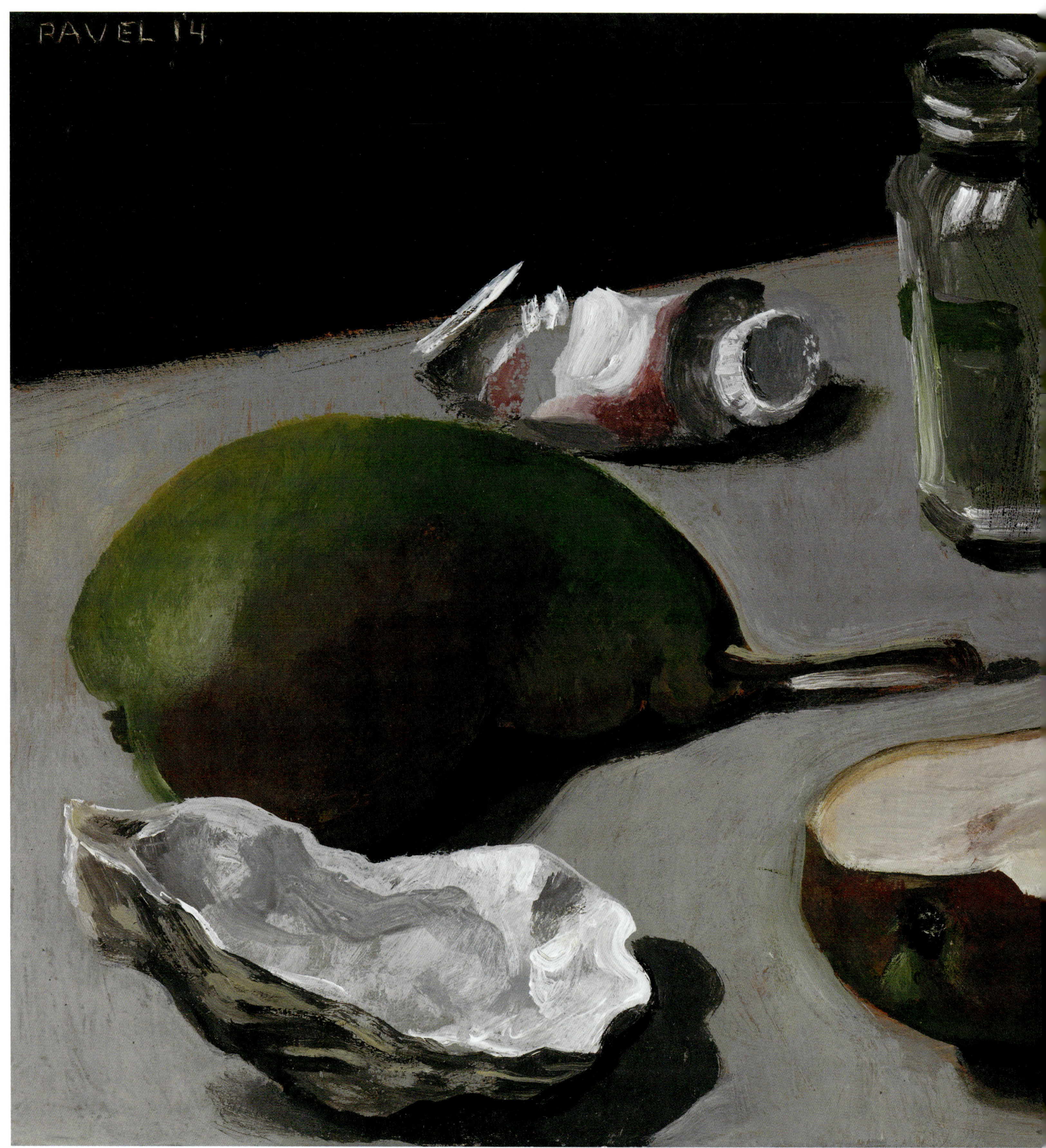
PAVEL 14

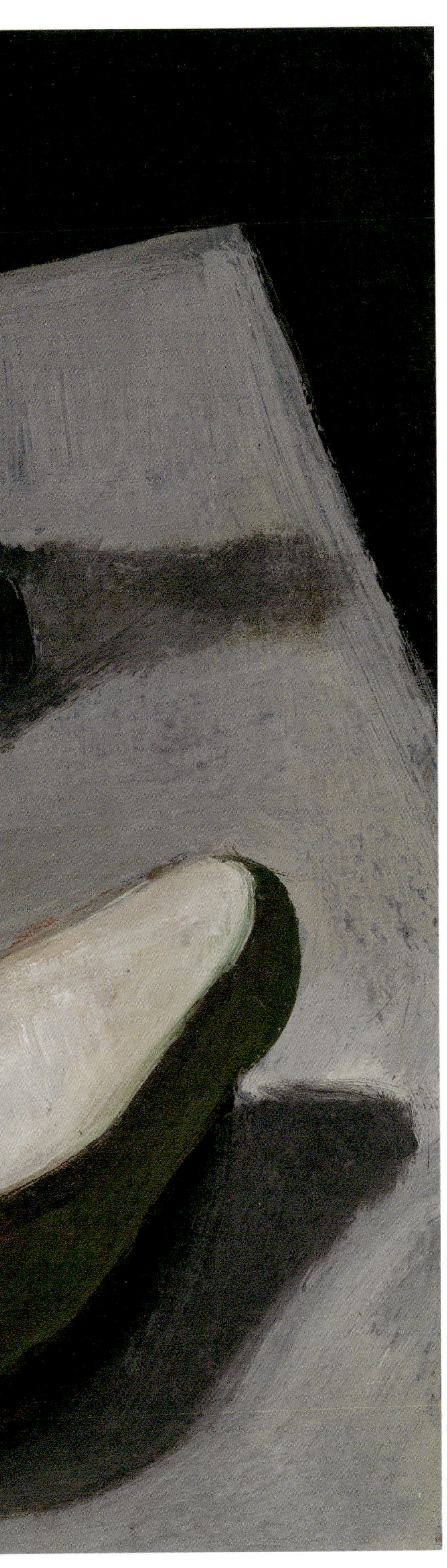

1944, **Tempera auf Hartfaser** / Tempera on hardboard, **24 × 30 cm, 2014**

1699, **Tempera auf Hartfaser** / Tempera on hardboard, **30 × 30 cm, 2013**

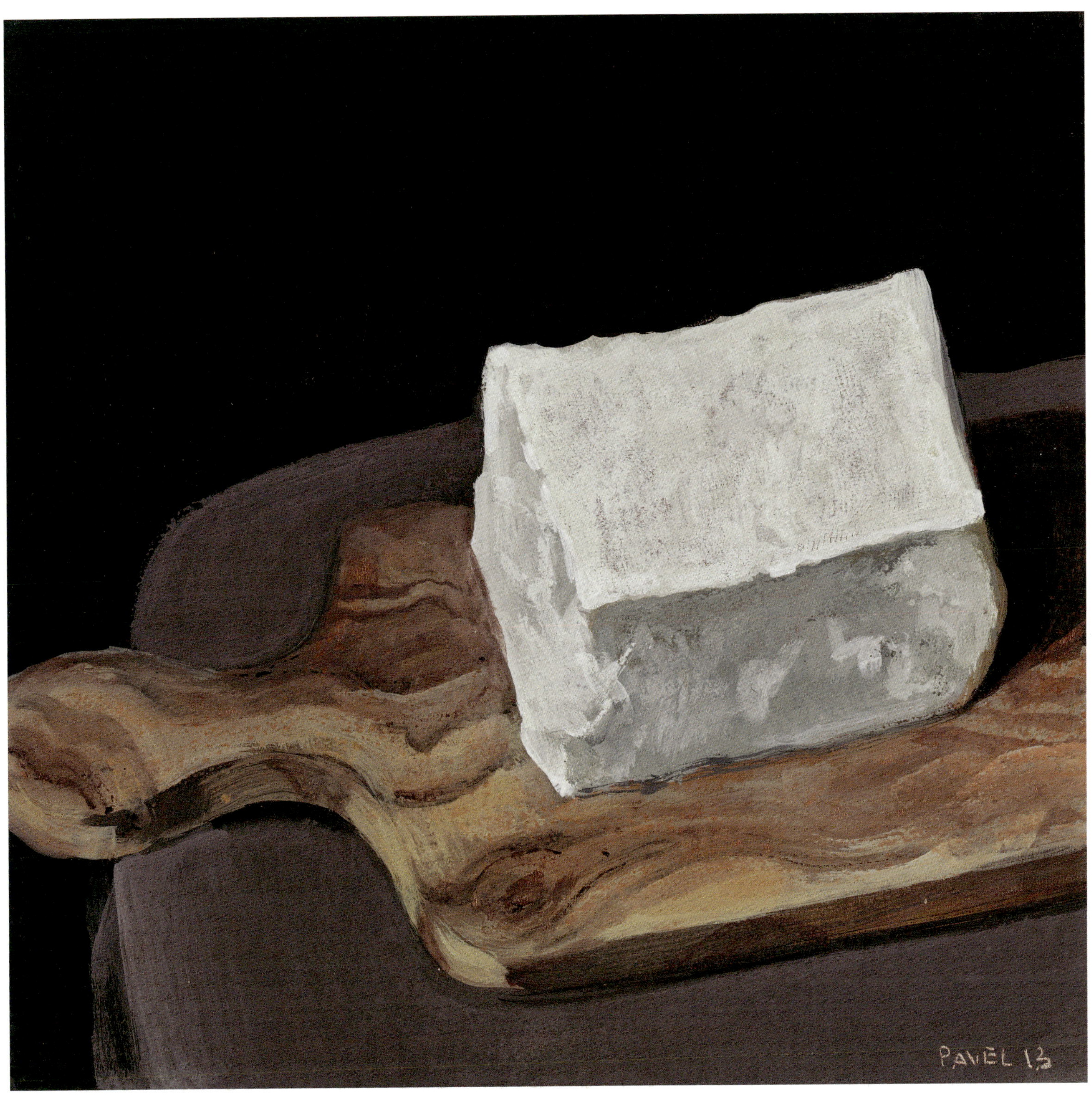
PAVEL 13

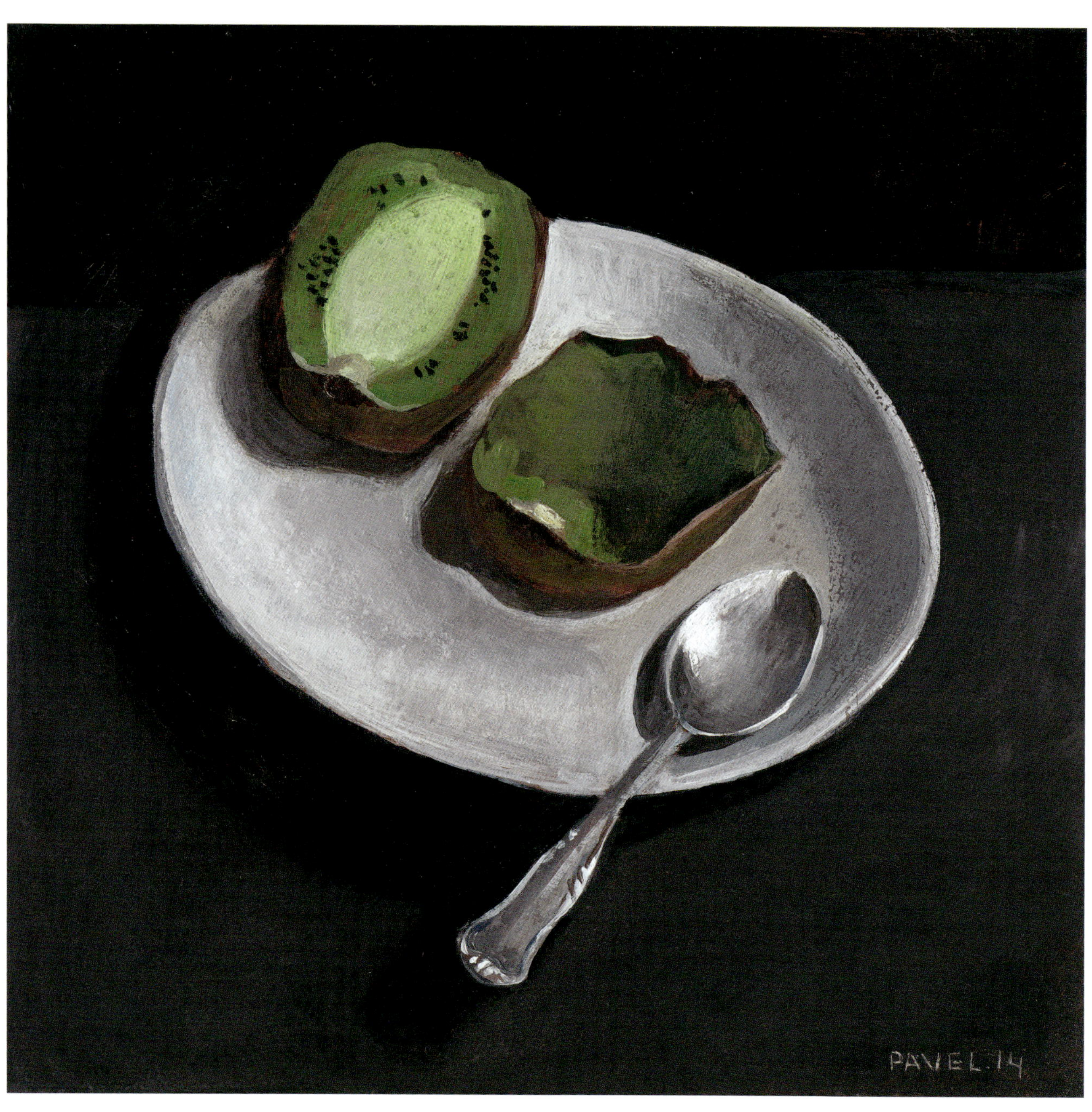

1967, **Tempera auf Hartfaser** / Tempera on hardboard, 30 × 30 cm, 2014

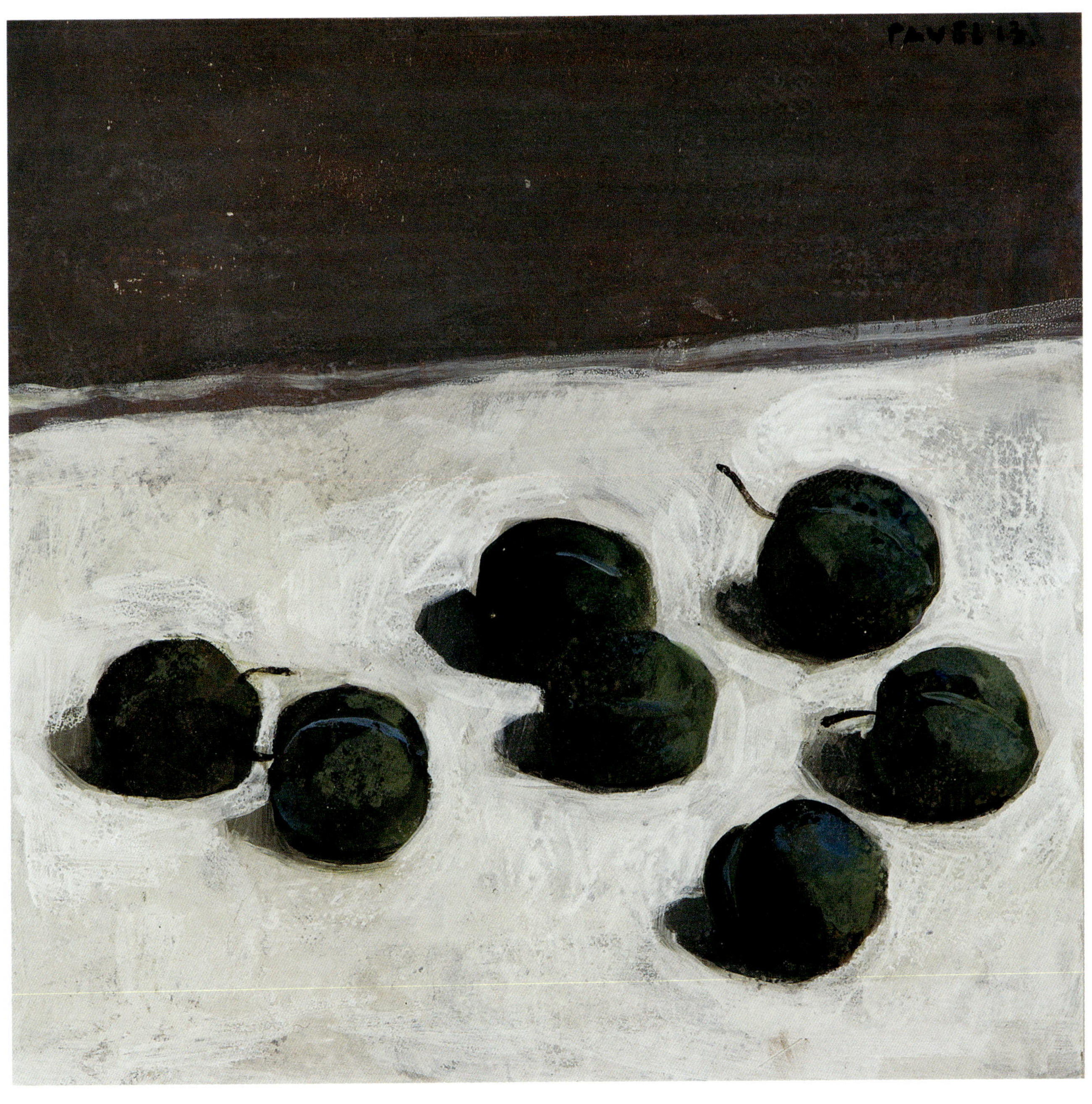

1785, **Tempera auf Hartfaser** / Tempera on hardboard, 30 × 30 cm, 2013

1851, **Tempera auf Hartfaser** / Tempera on hardboard, 30 × 30 cm, 2014

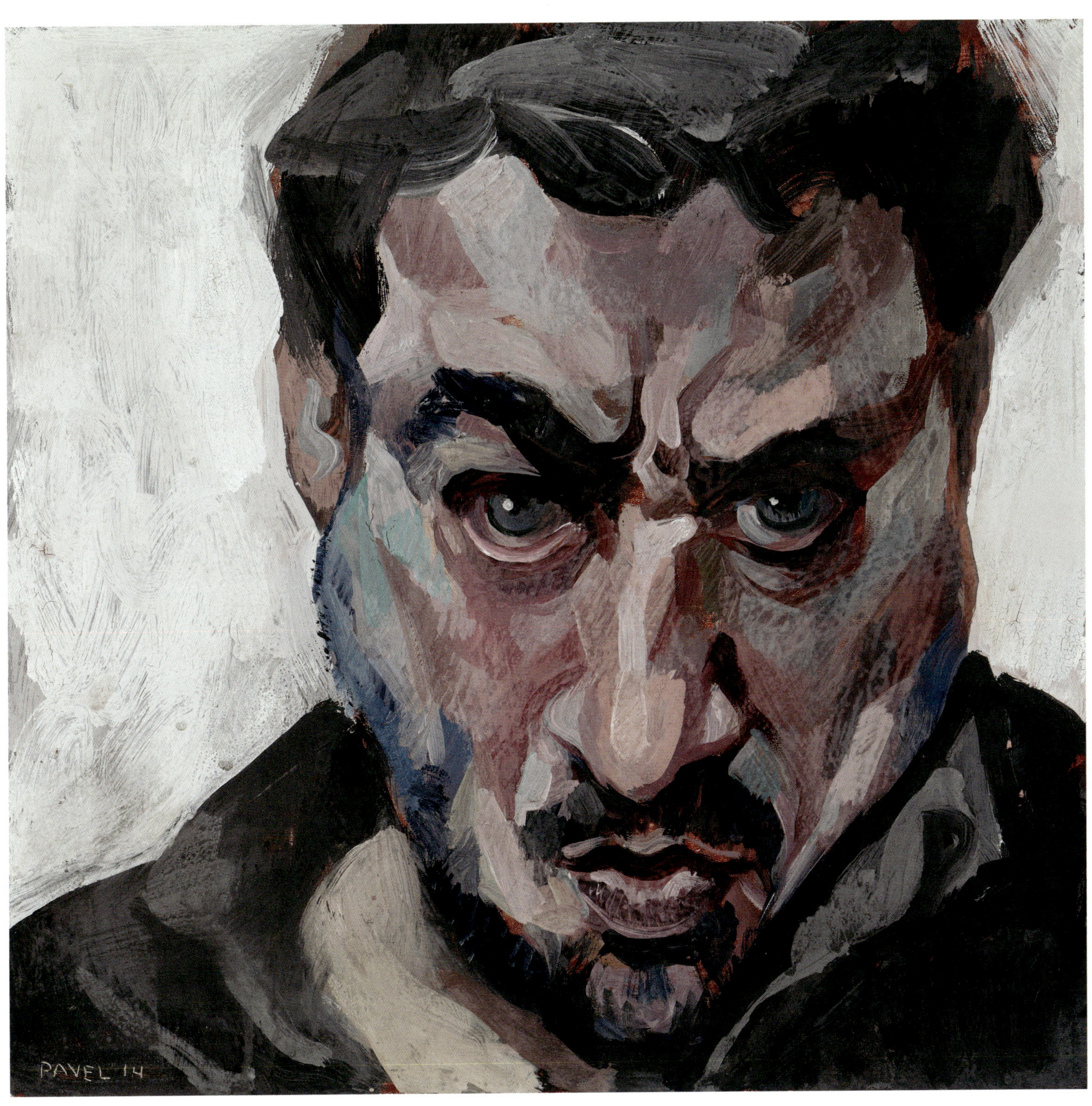
PAVEL 14

1966, **Tempera auf Hartfaser** / Tempera on hardboard, 30 × 30 cm, 2014

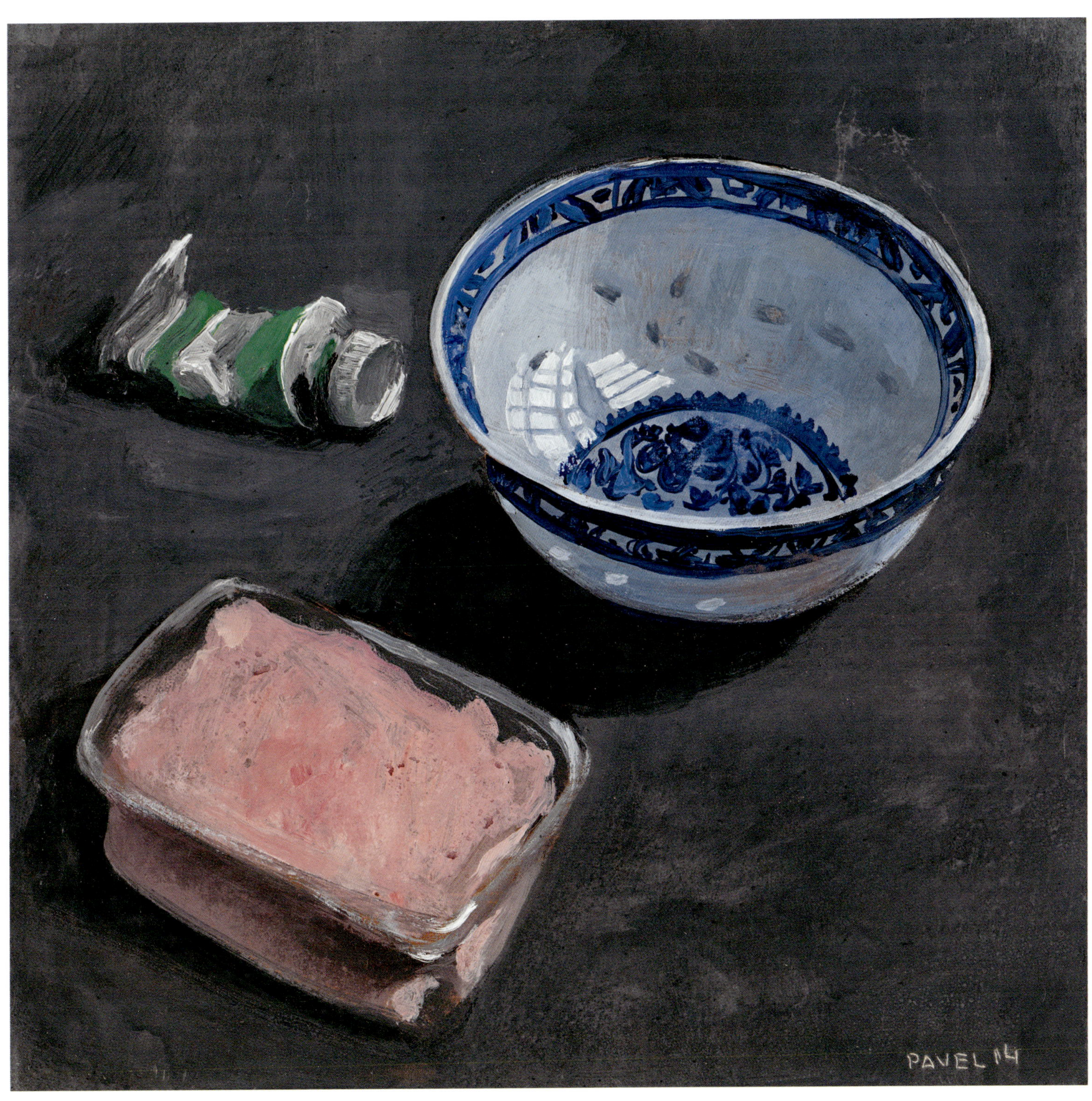
PAVEL 14

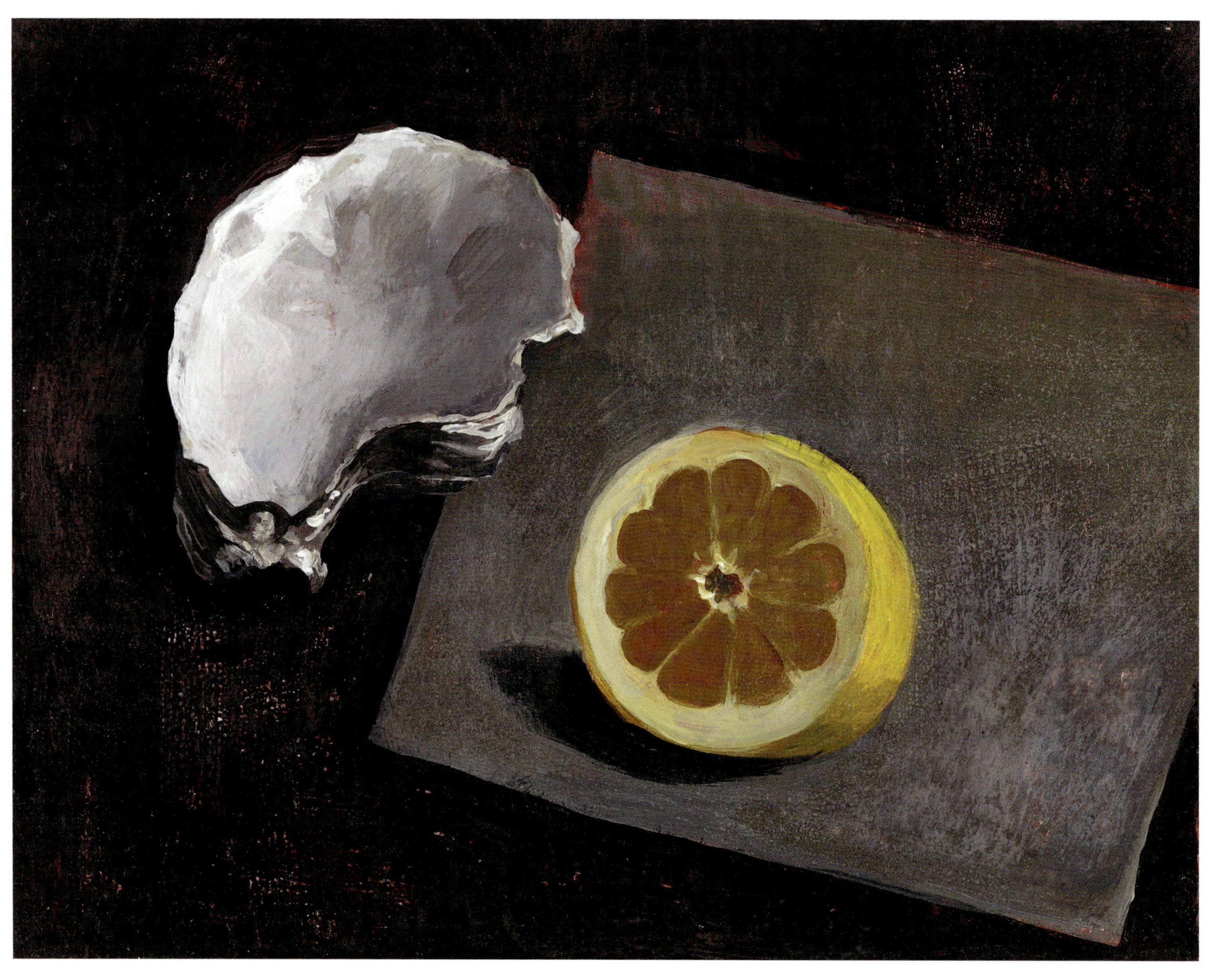

1868, **Tempera auf Hartfaser** / Tempera on hardboard, **24 × 30 cm, 2014**

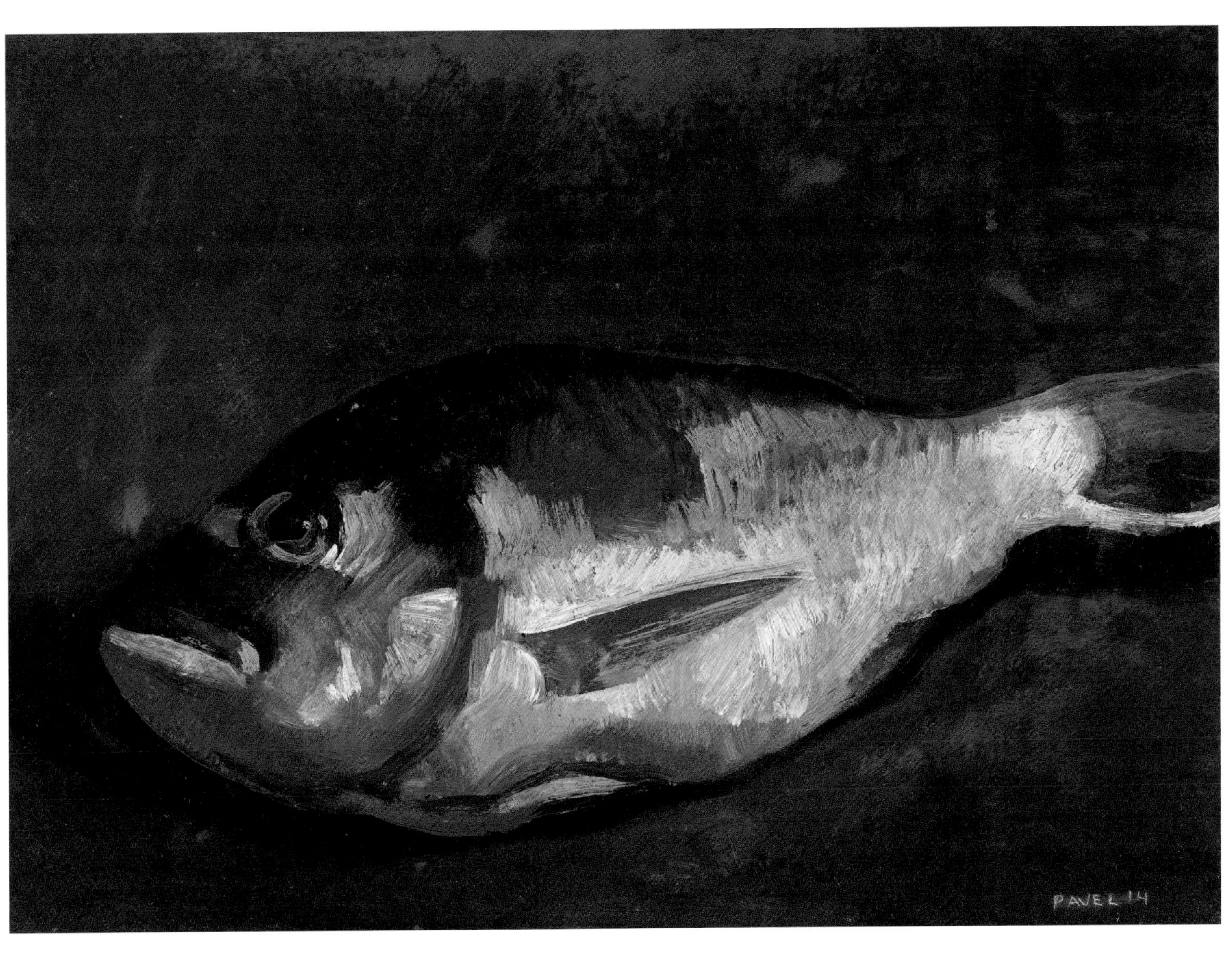

1959, **Tempera auf Hartfaser** / Tempera on hardboard, 30 × 40 cm, 2014

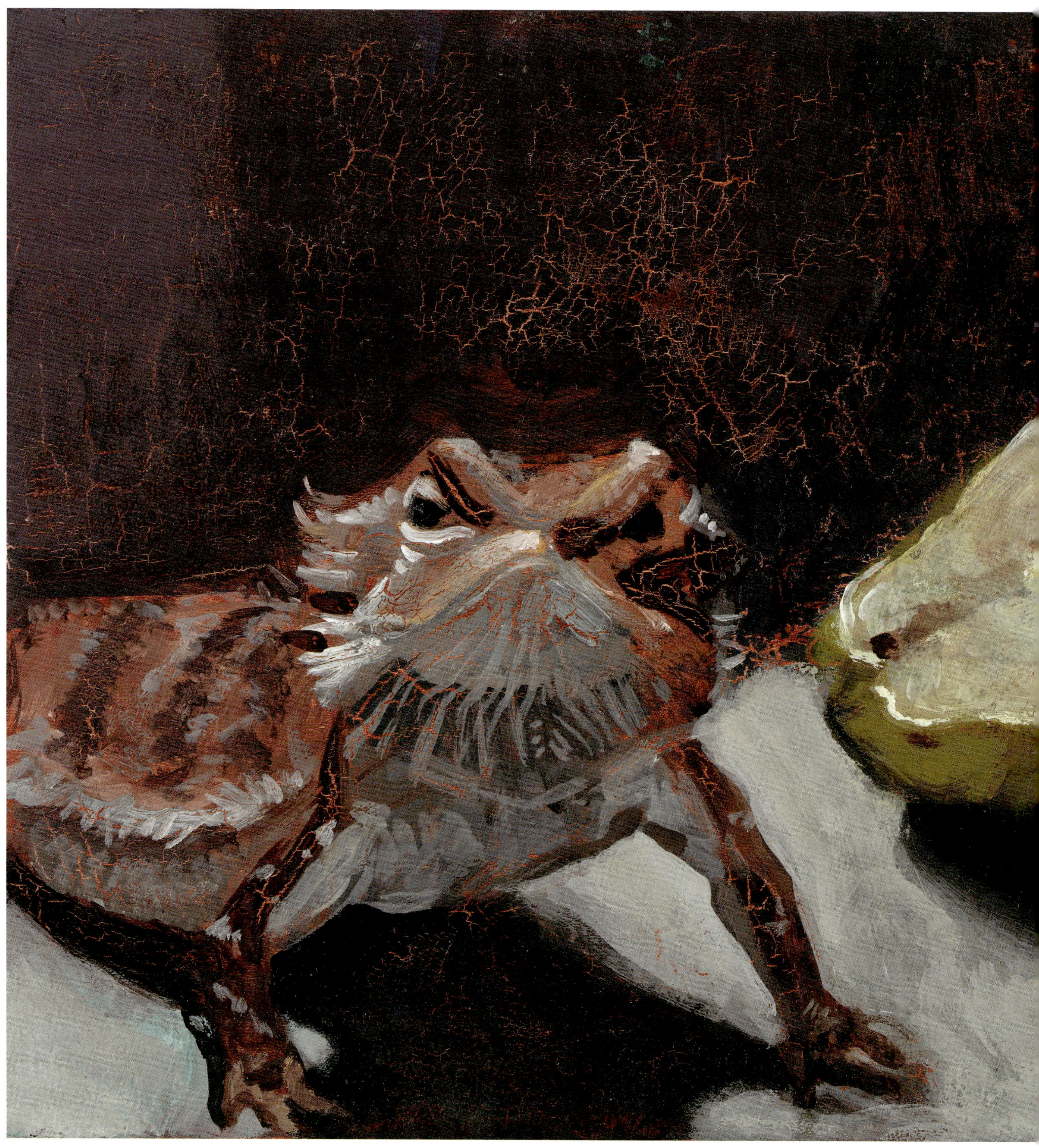

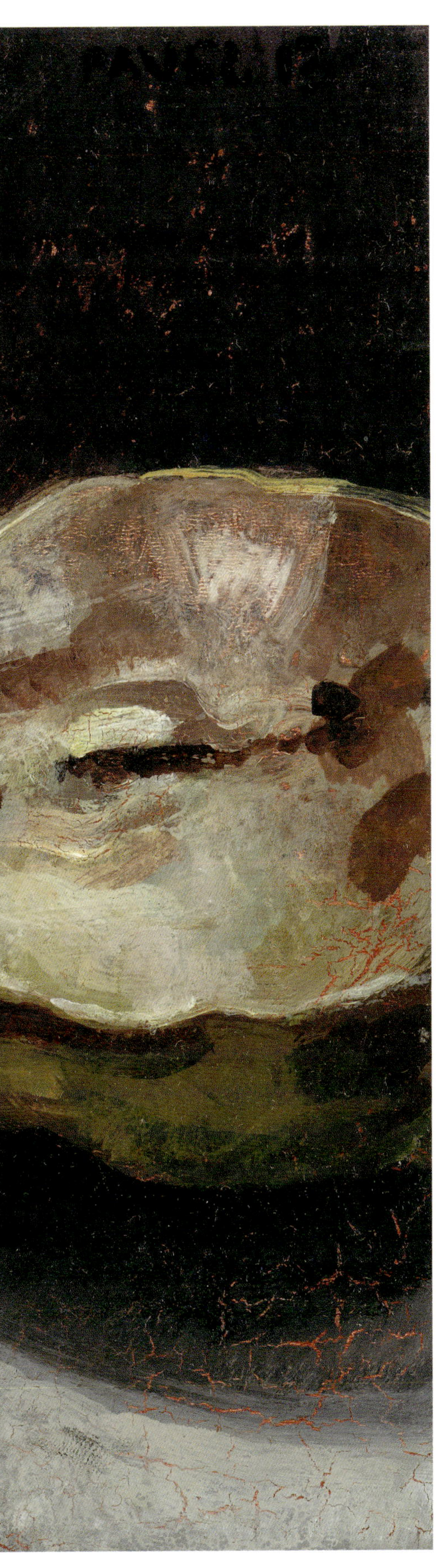

1815, **Tempera auf Hartfaser** / Tempera on hardboard, **24 × 30 cm, 2013**

1810, **Tempera auf Hartfaser** / Tempera on hardboard, 30 × 30 cm, 2013

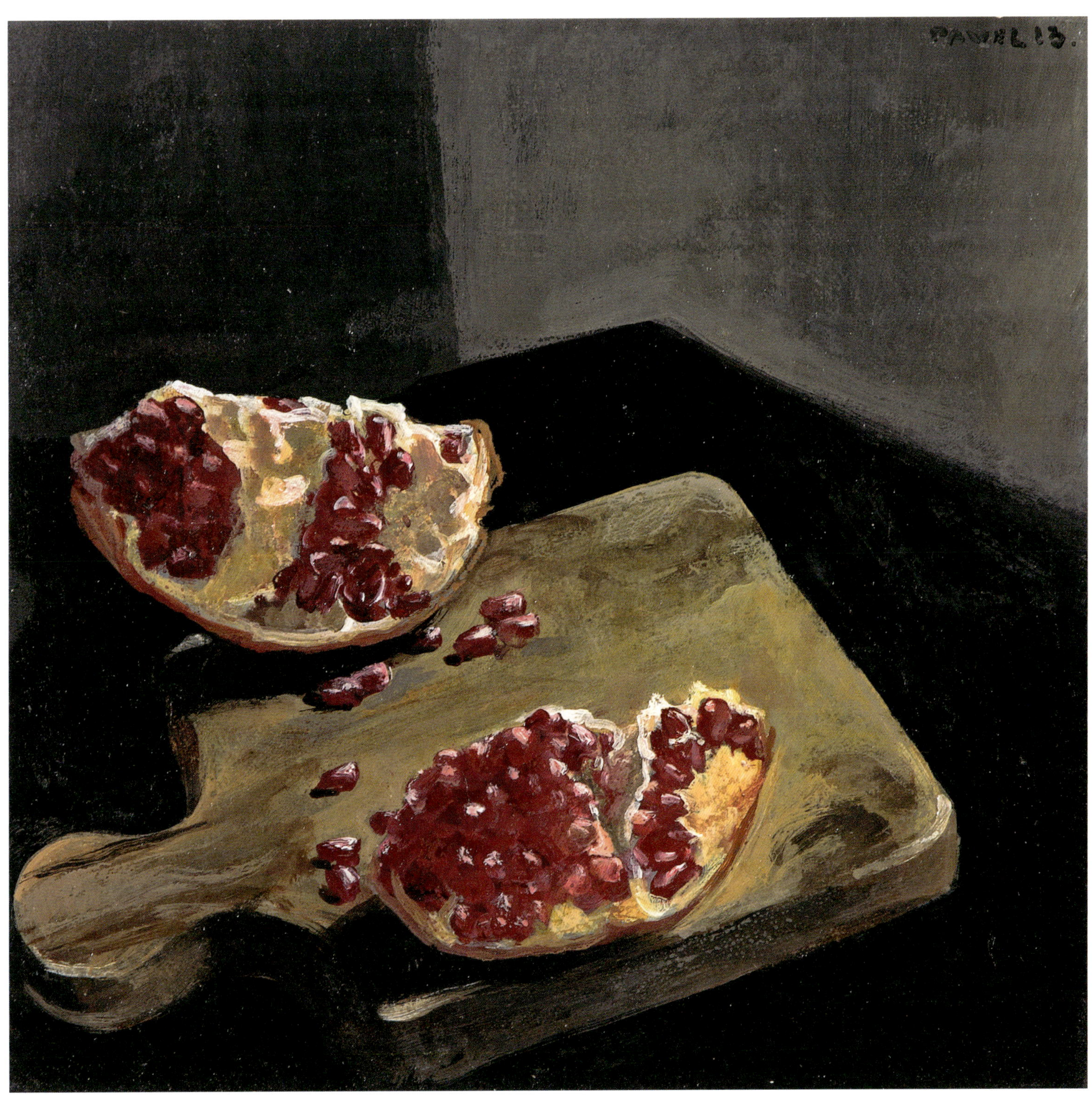

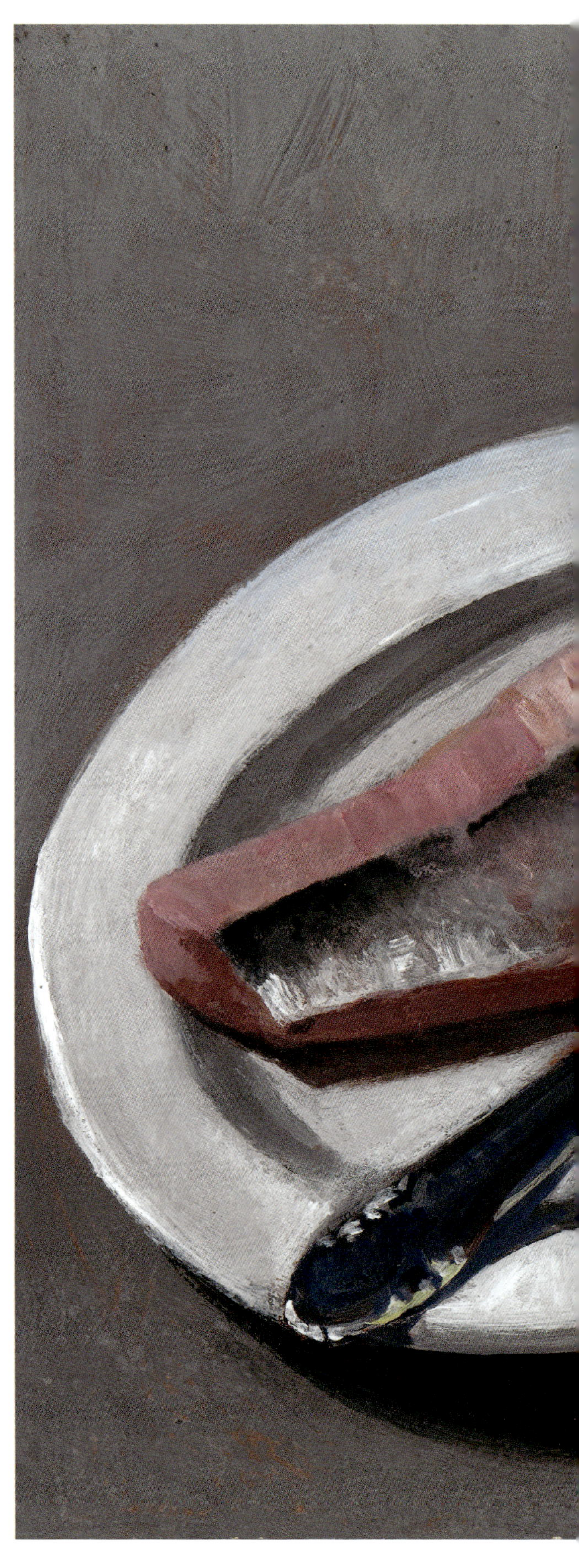

1946, **Tempera auf Hartfaser** / Tempera on hardboard, **30 × 40 cm, 2014**

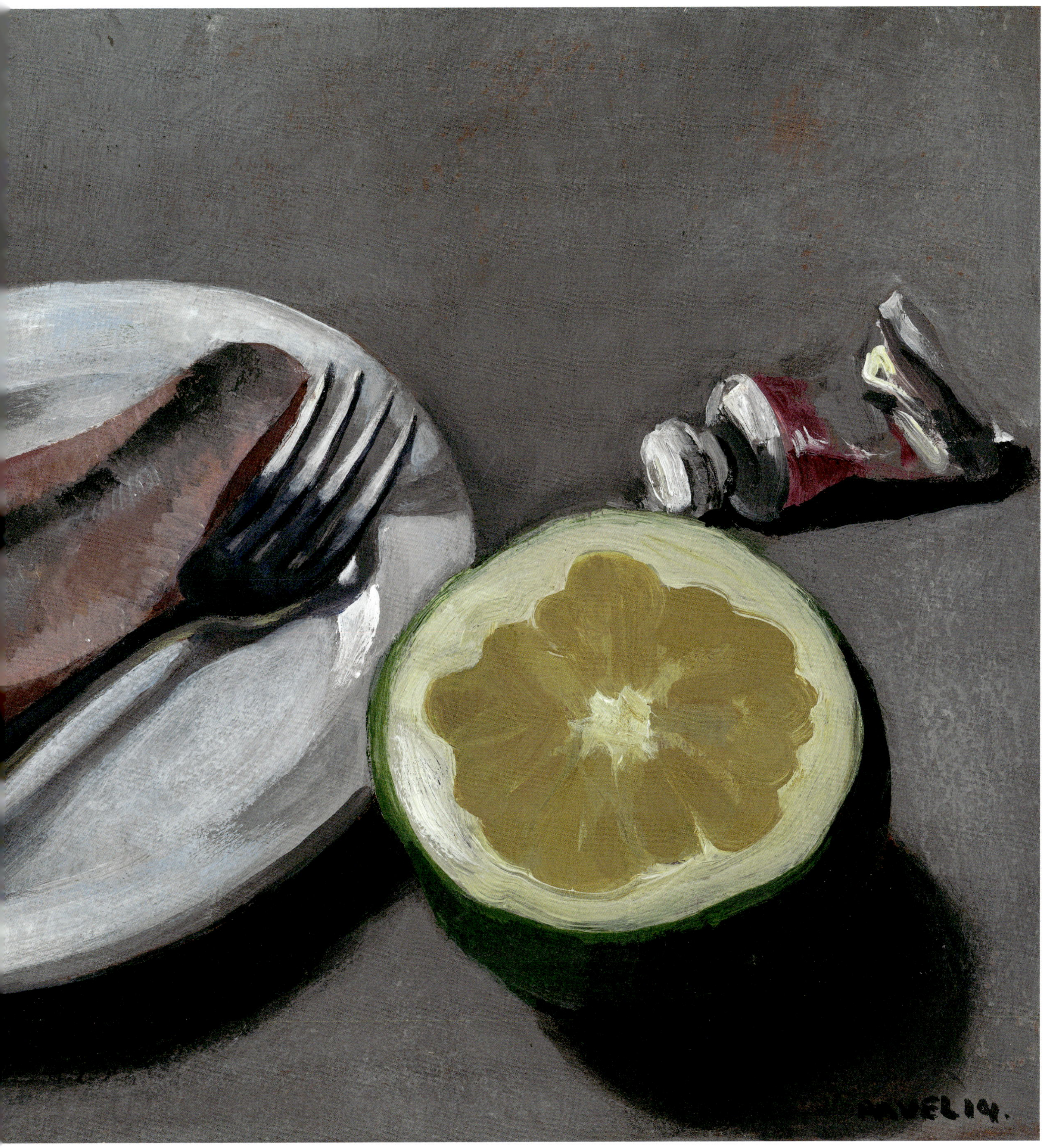

1706, **Tempera auf Hartfaser** / Tempera on hardboard, 30 × 30 cm, 2013

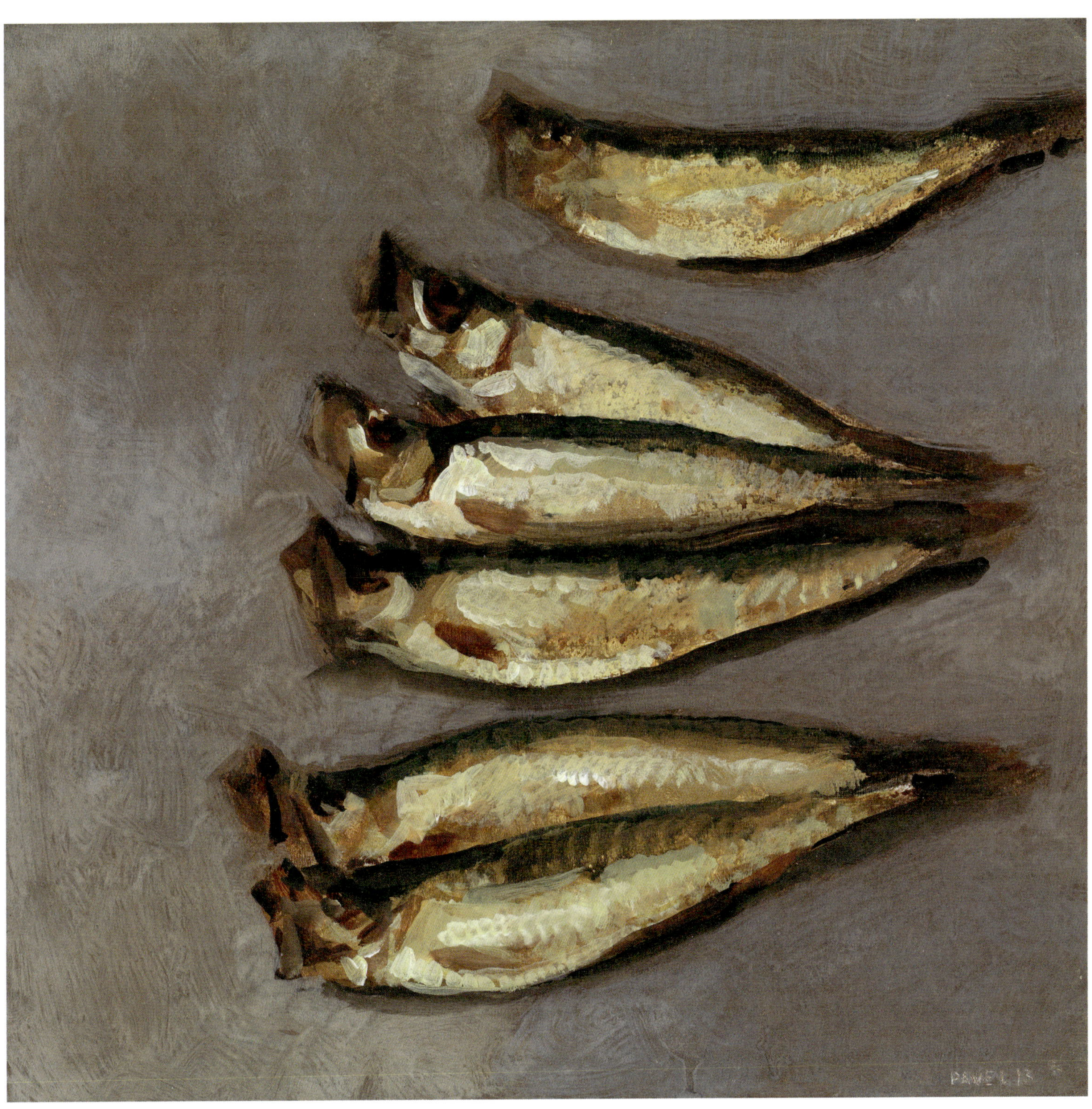
PAVEL 13

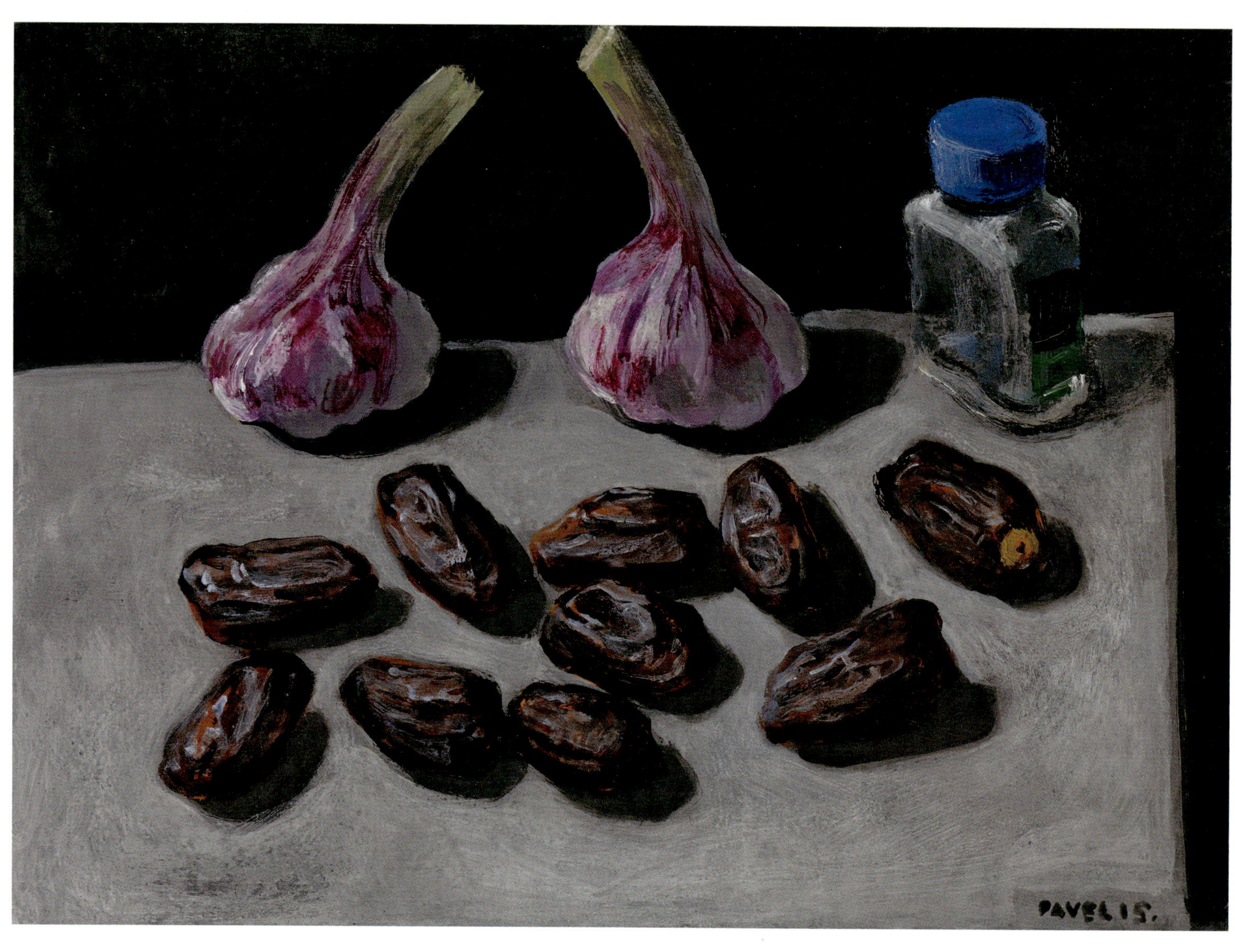

1979, **Tempera auf Hartfaser** / Tempera on hardboard, 30 × 40 cm, 2015

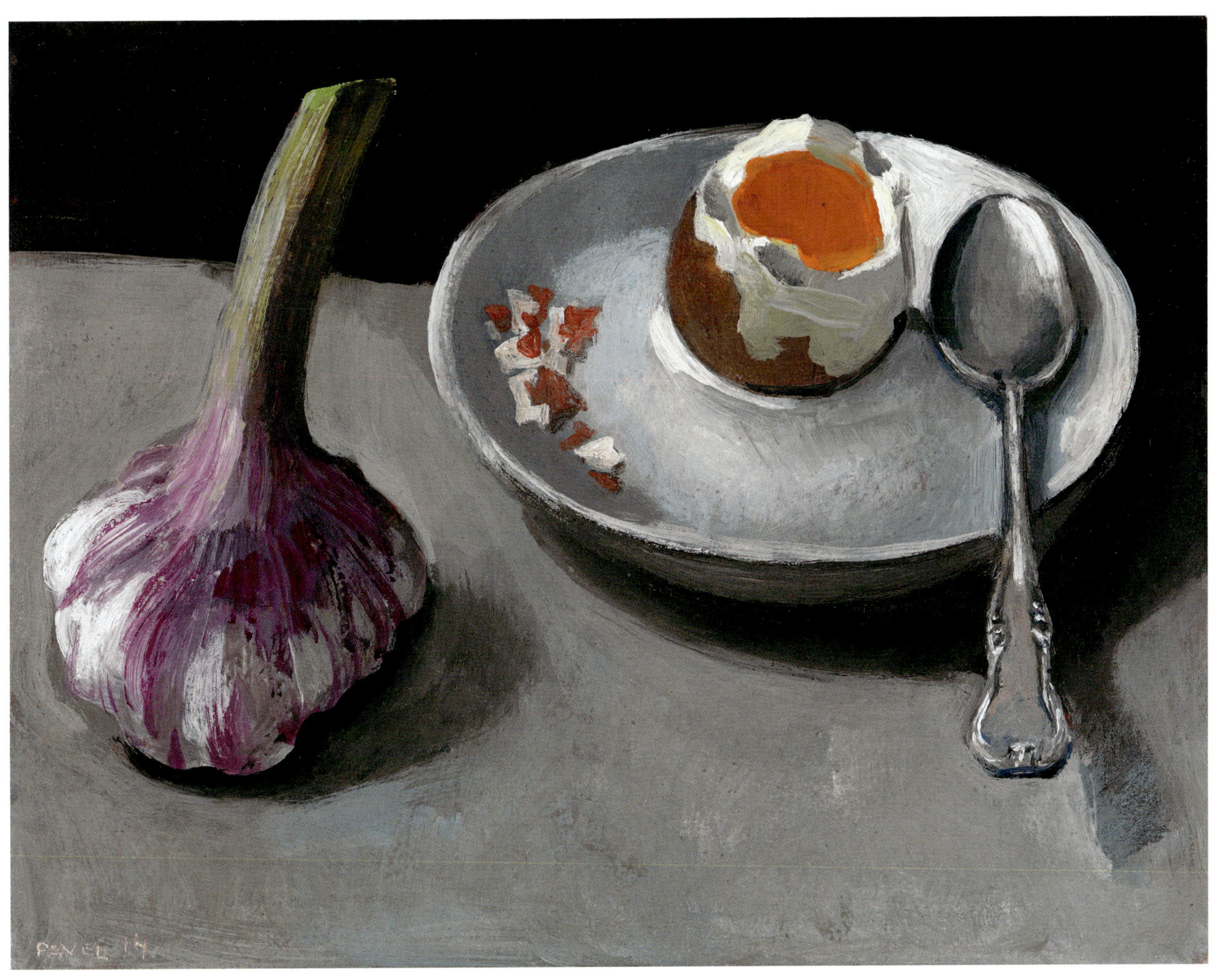

1939, Tempera auf Hartfaser / Tempera on hardboard, 24 × 30 cm, 2014

1836, **Tempera auf Hartfaser** / Tempera on hardboard, 40 × 30 cm, 2014

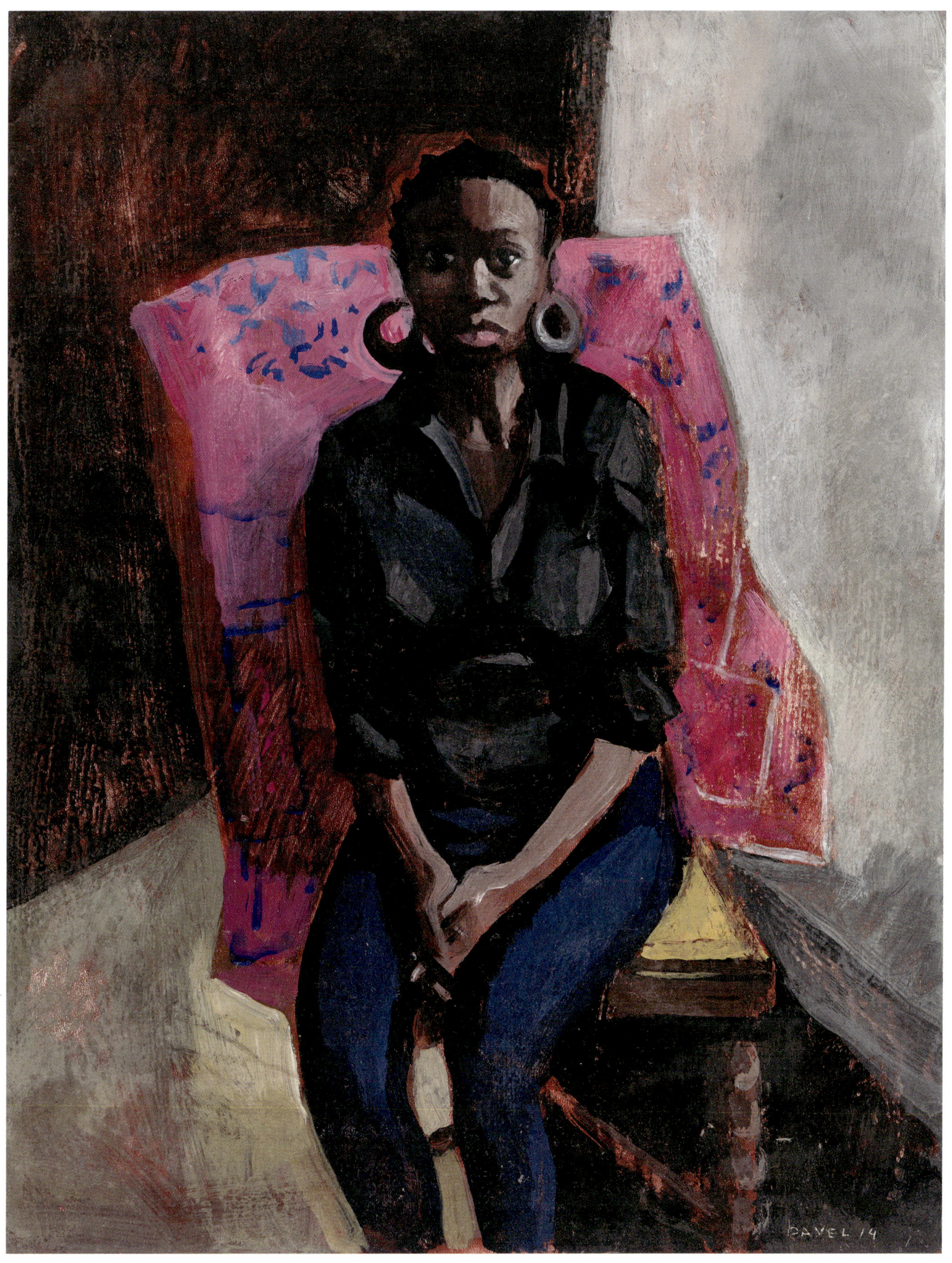
PAVEL 14

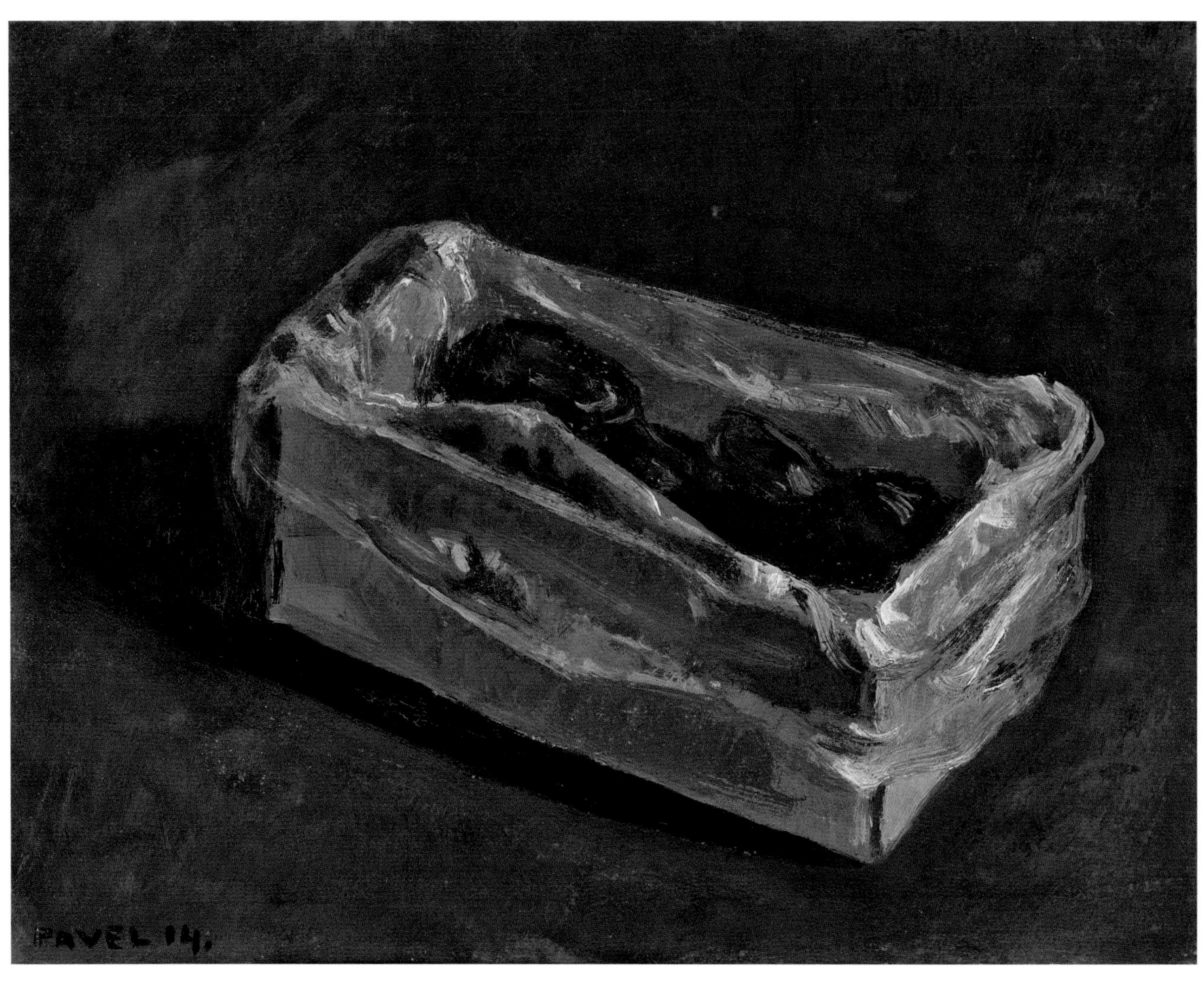

1960, **Tempera auf Hartfaser** / Tempera on hardboard, **24 × 30 cm, 2014**

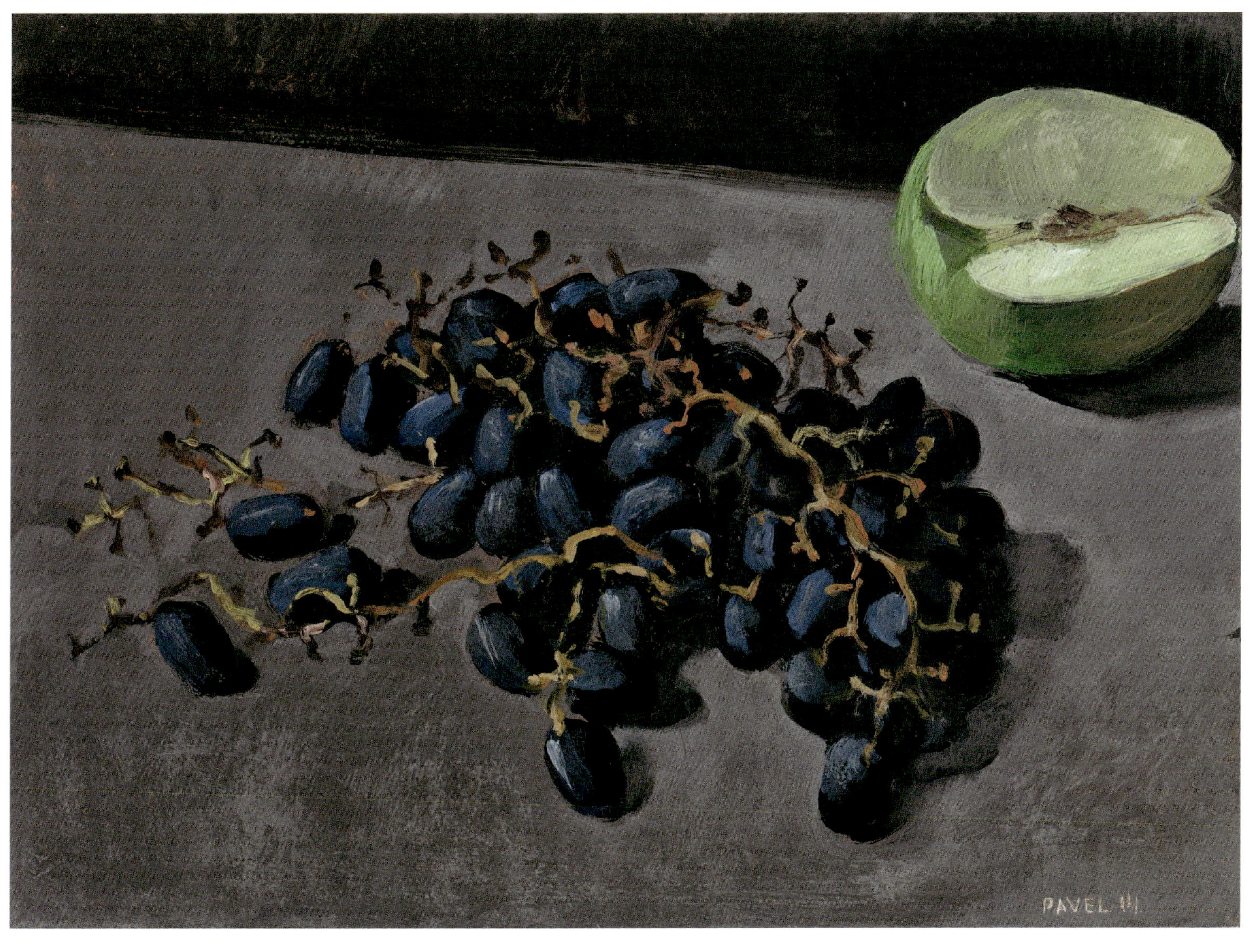

1961, **Tempera auf Hartfaser** / Tempera on hardboard, 30 × 40 cm, 2014

1805, **Tempera auf Hartfaser** / Tempera on hardboard, 30 × 30 cm, 2013

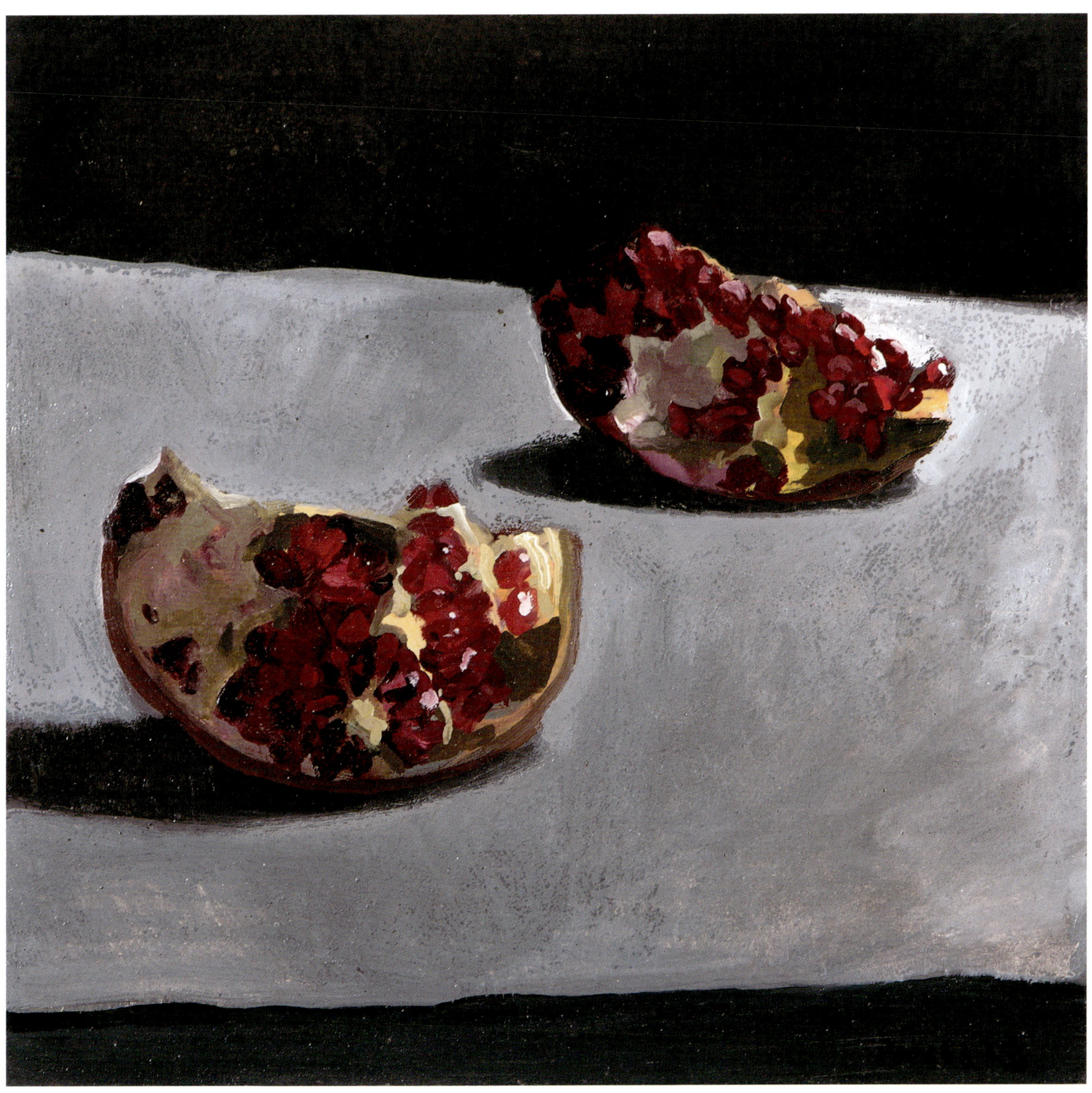

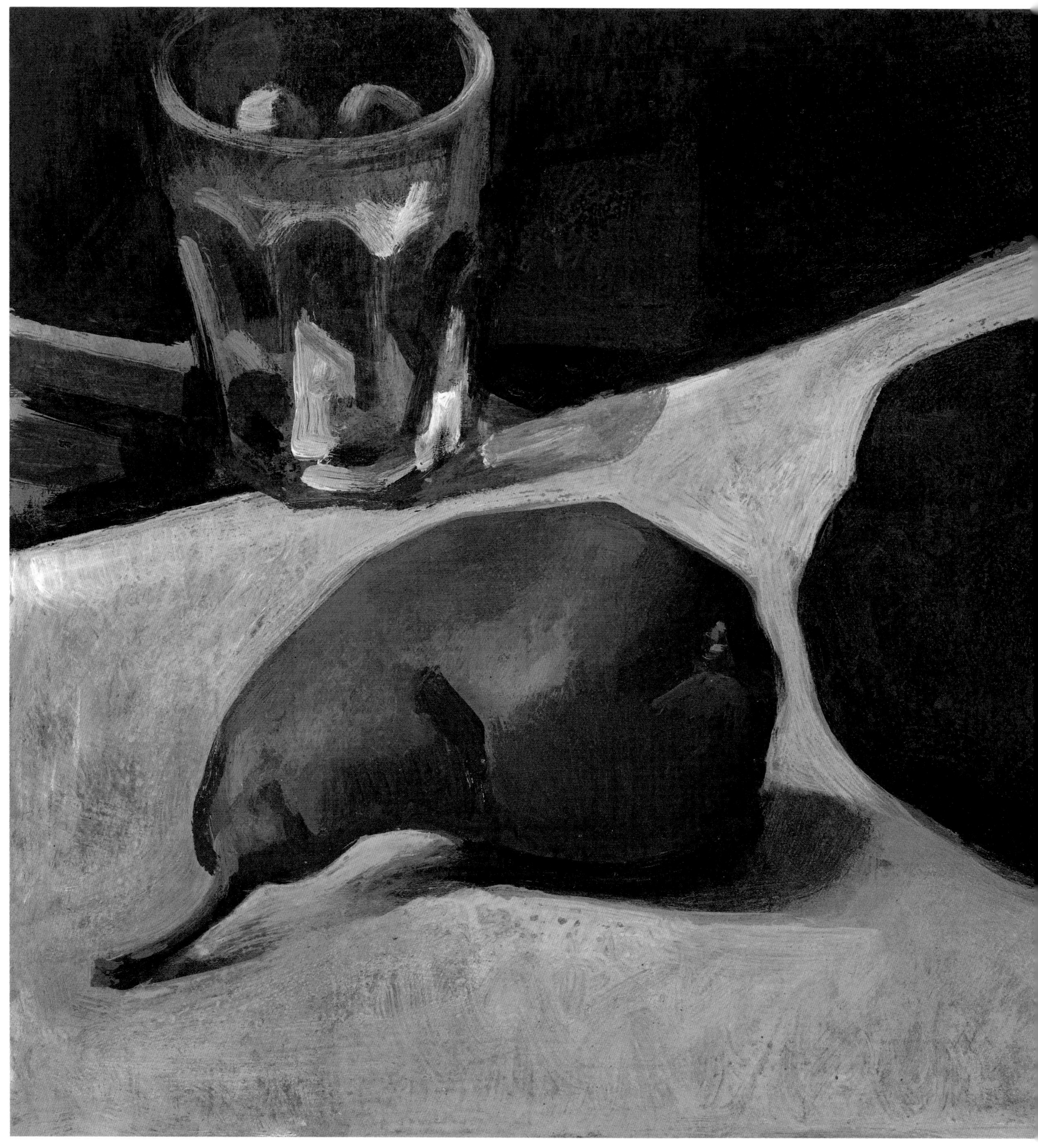

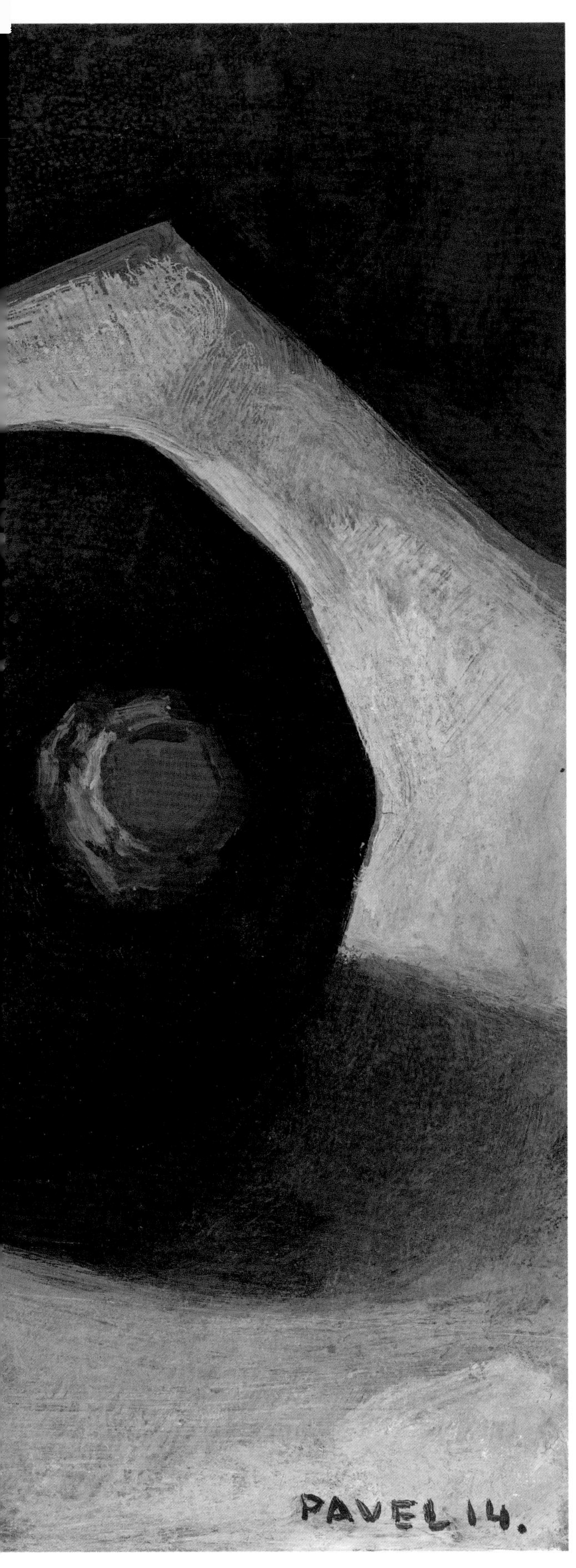

1943, **Tempera auf Hartfaser** / Tempera on hardboard, 30 × 40 cm, 2014

1702, **Tempera auf Hartfaser** / Tempera on hardboard, **40 × 30 cm**, 2013

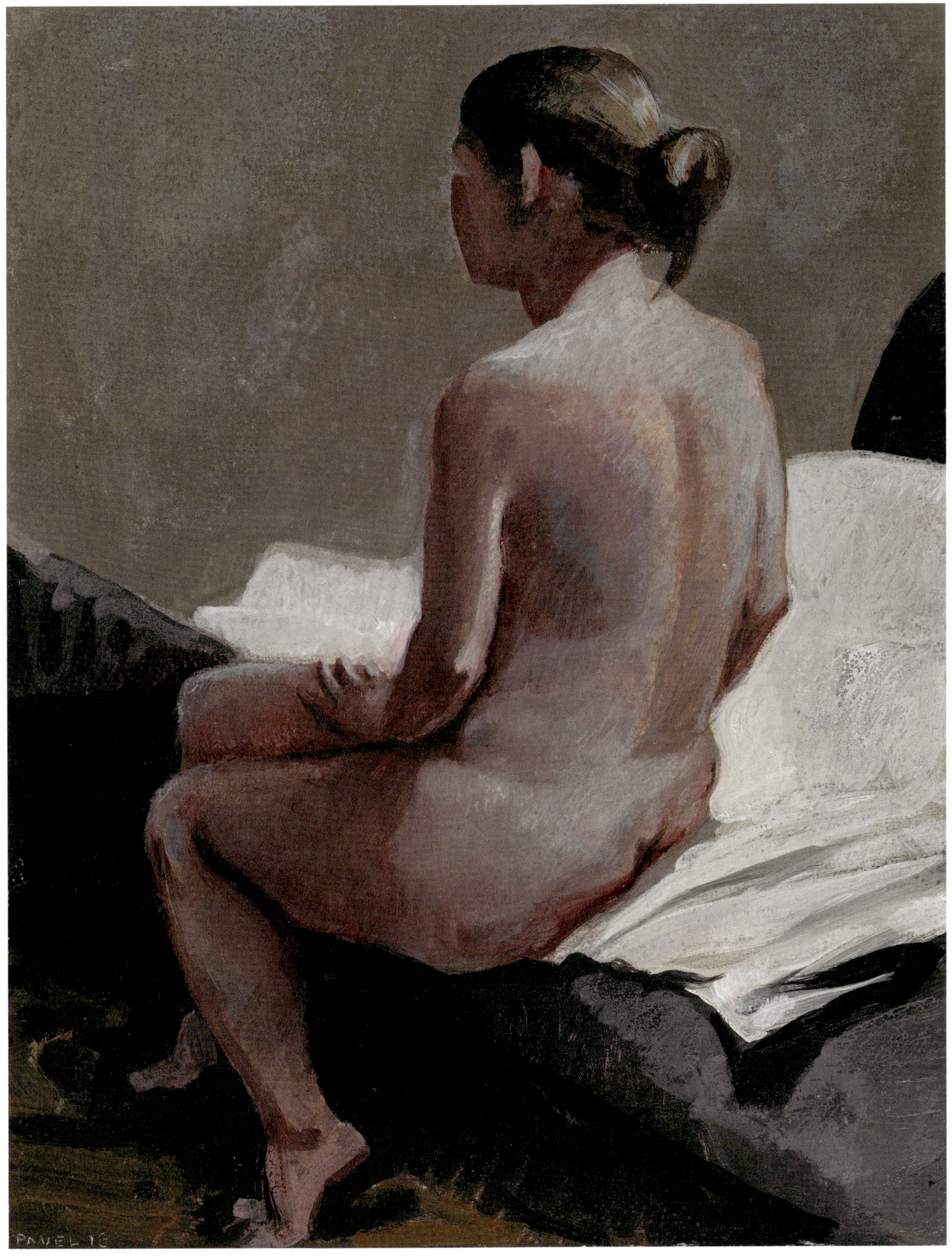
PAVEL 16

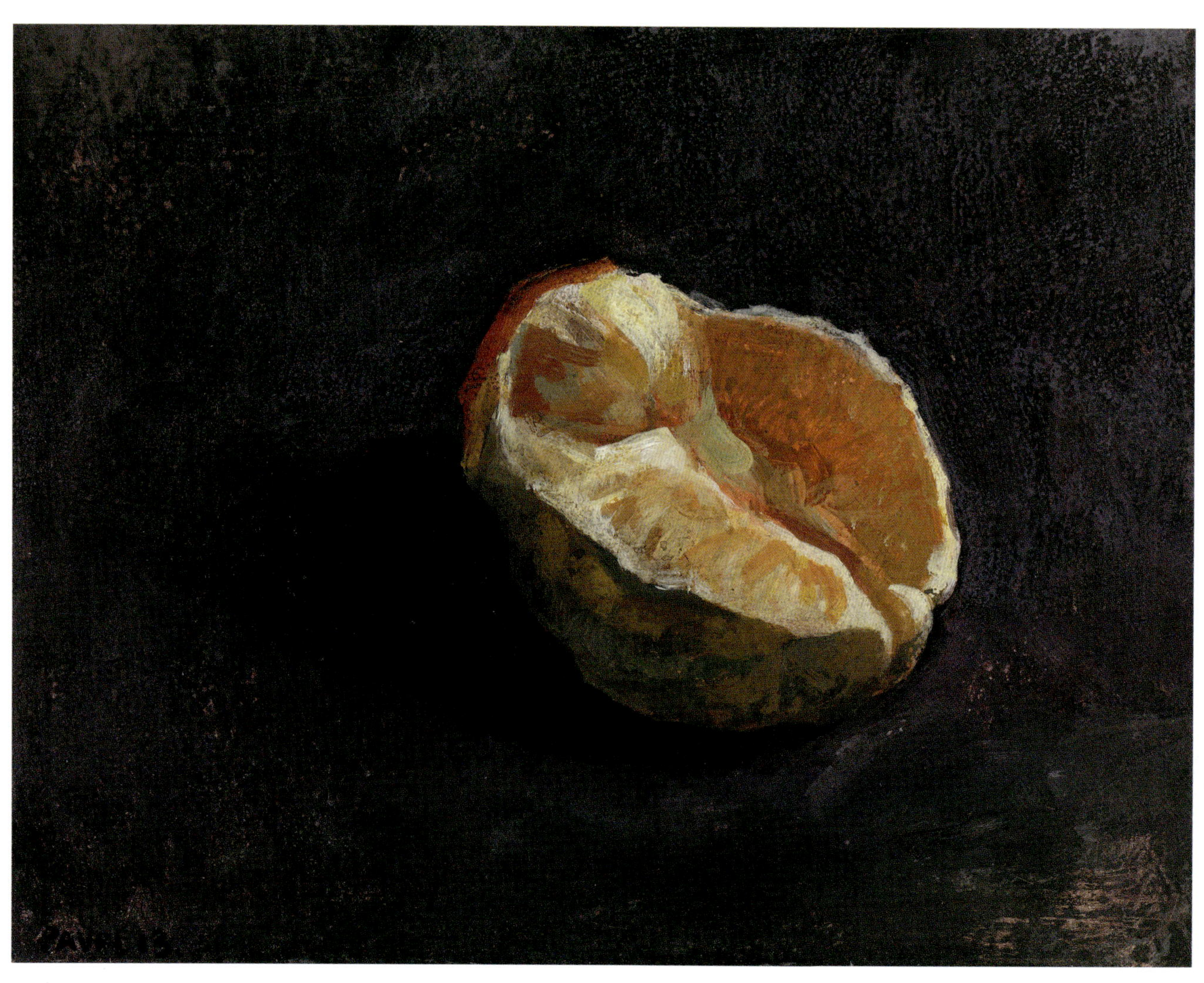

1812, **Tempera auf Hartfaser** / Tempera on hardboard, 24 × 30 cm, 2013

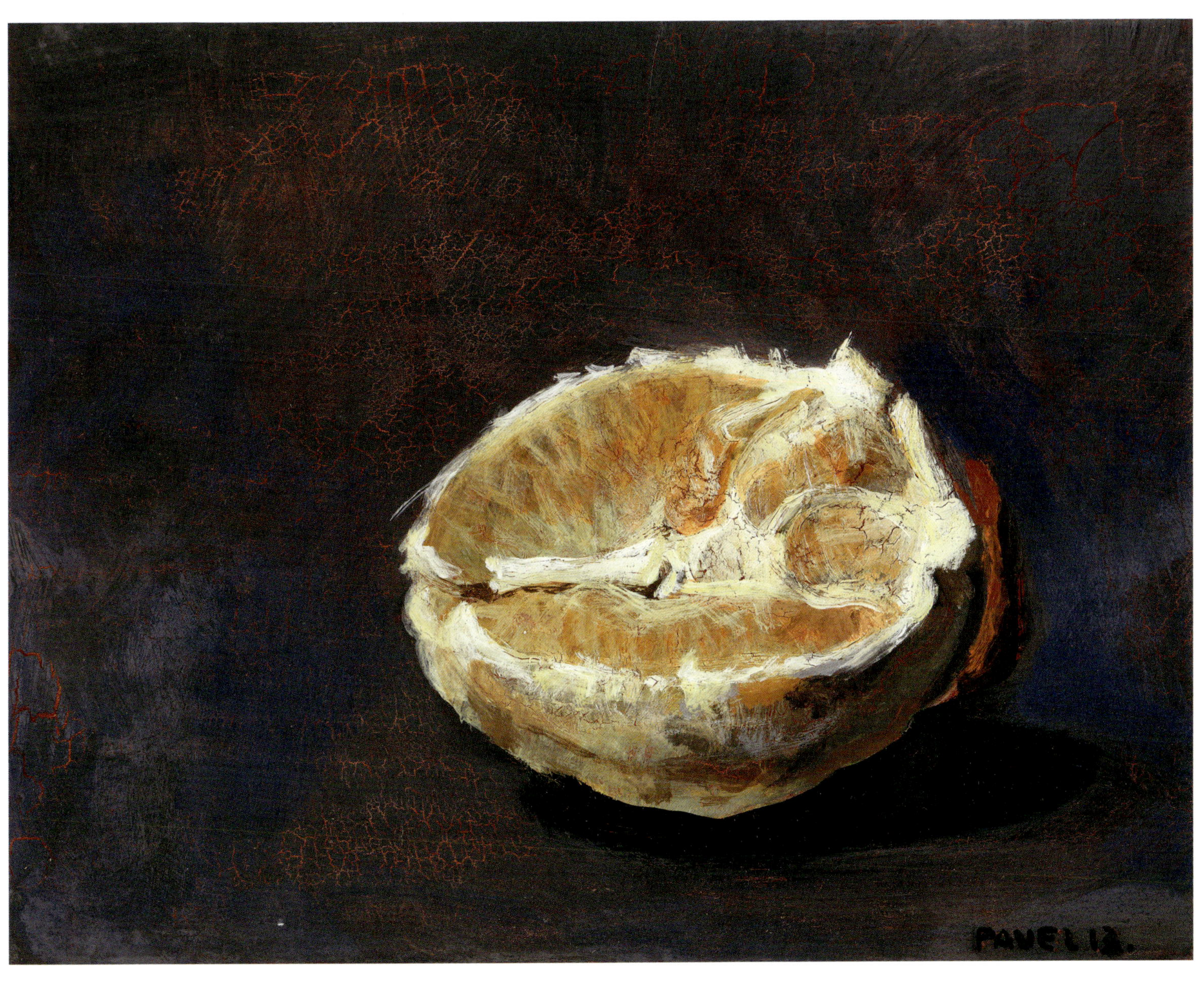

1816, **Tempera auf Hartfaser** / Tempera on hardboard, **24 × 30 cm, 2013**

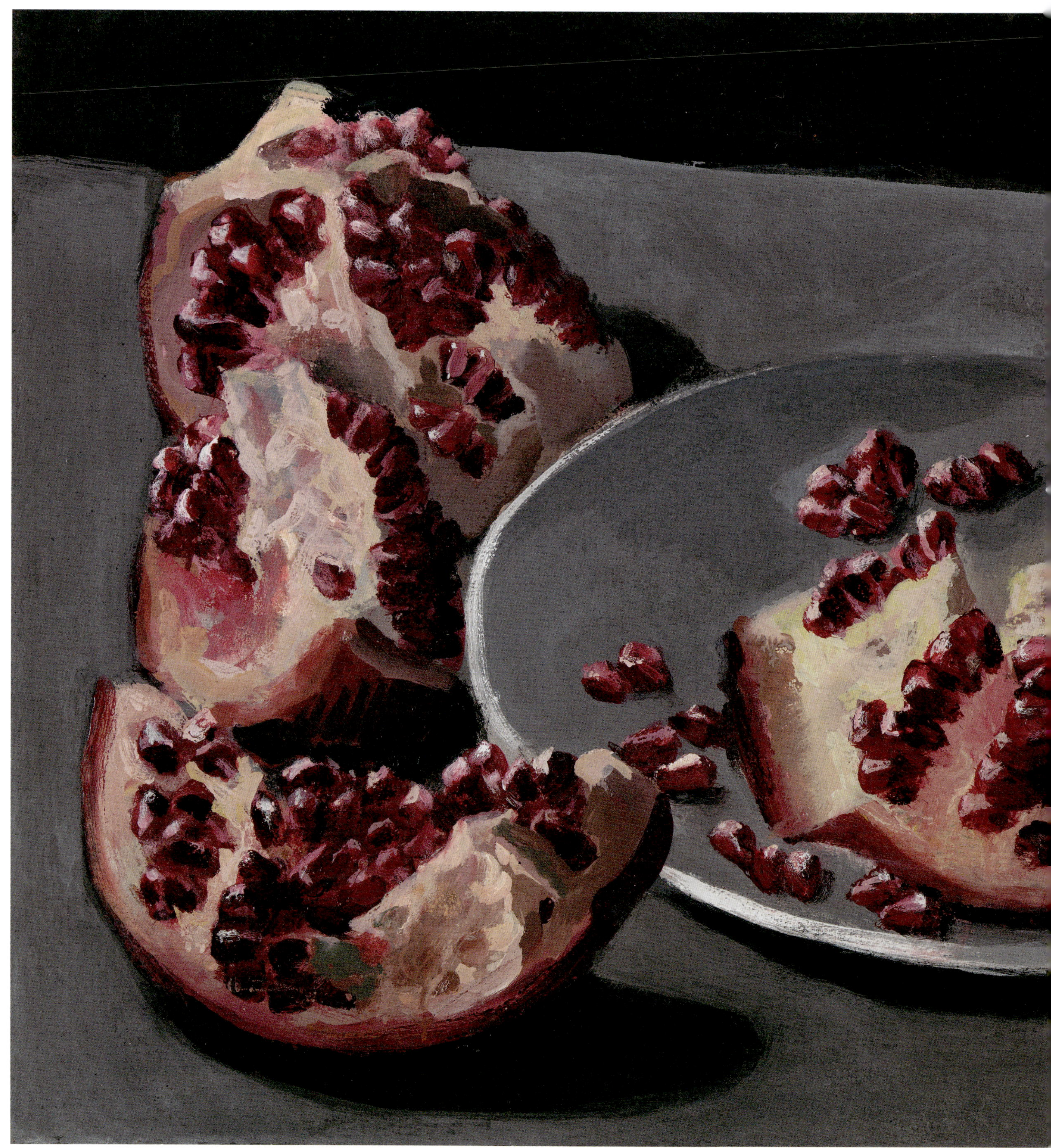

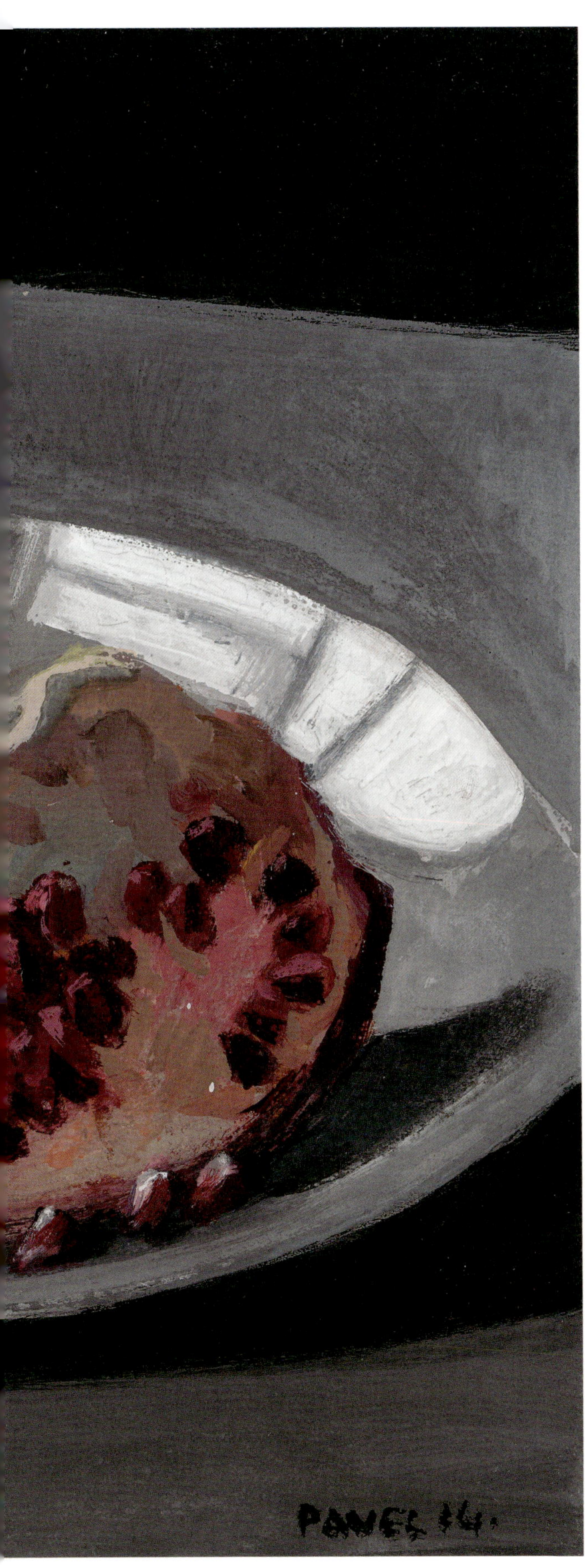

1950, **Tempera auf Hartfaser** / Tempera on hardboard, **30 × 40 cm, 2014**

1856, **Tempera auf Hartfaser** / Tempera on hardboard, **40 × 30 cm, 2014**

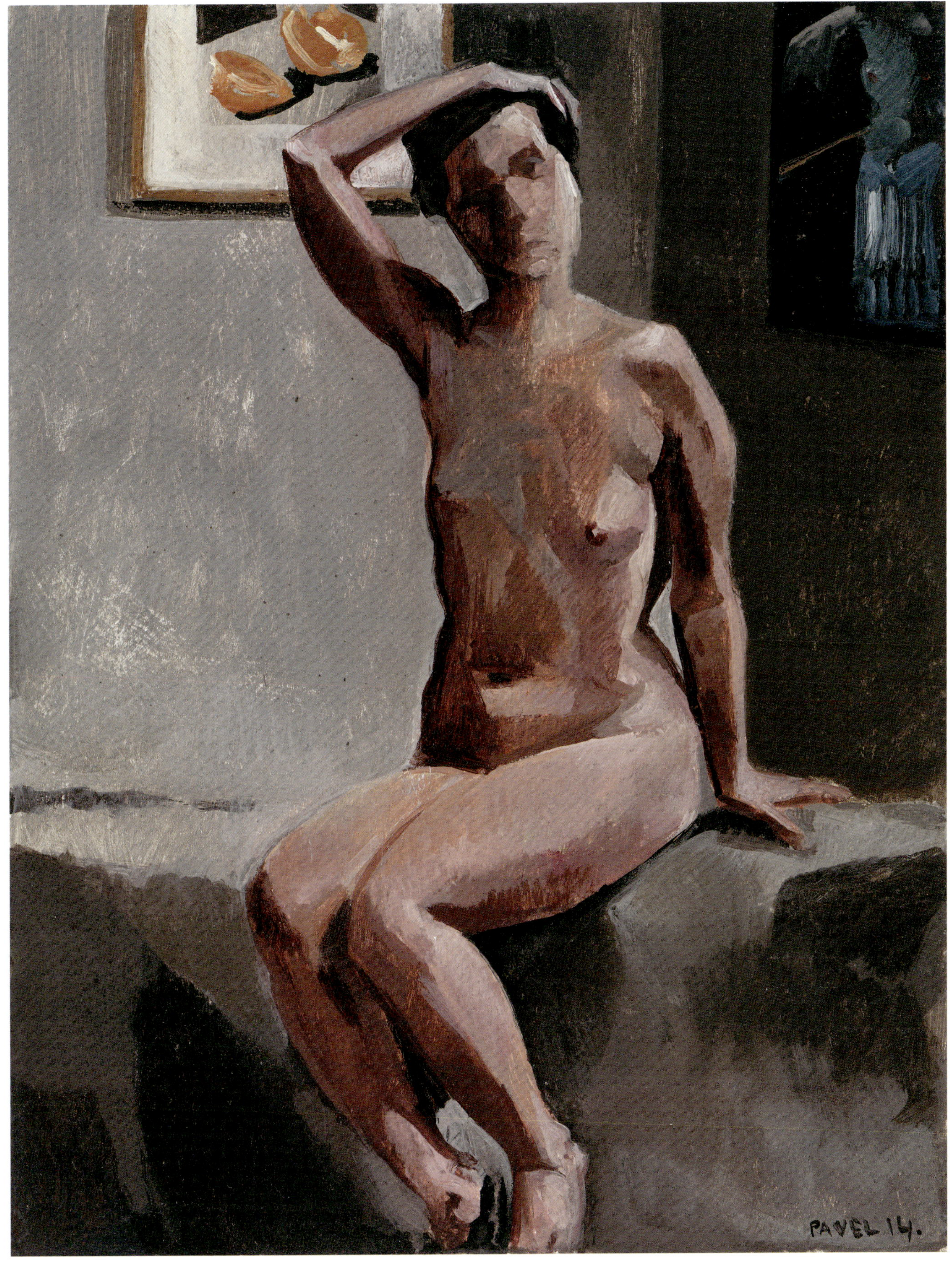
PAVEL 14.

1714, **Tempera auf Hartfaser** / Tempera on hardboard, 30 × 30 cm, 2013

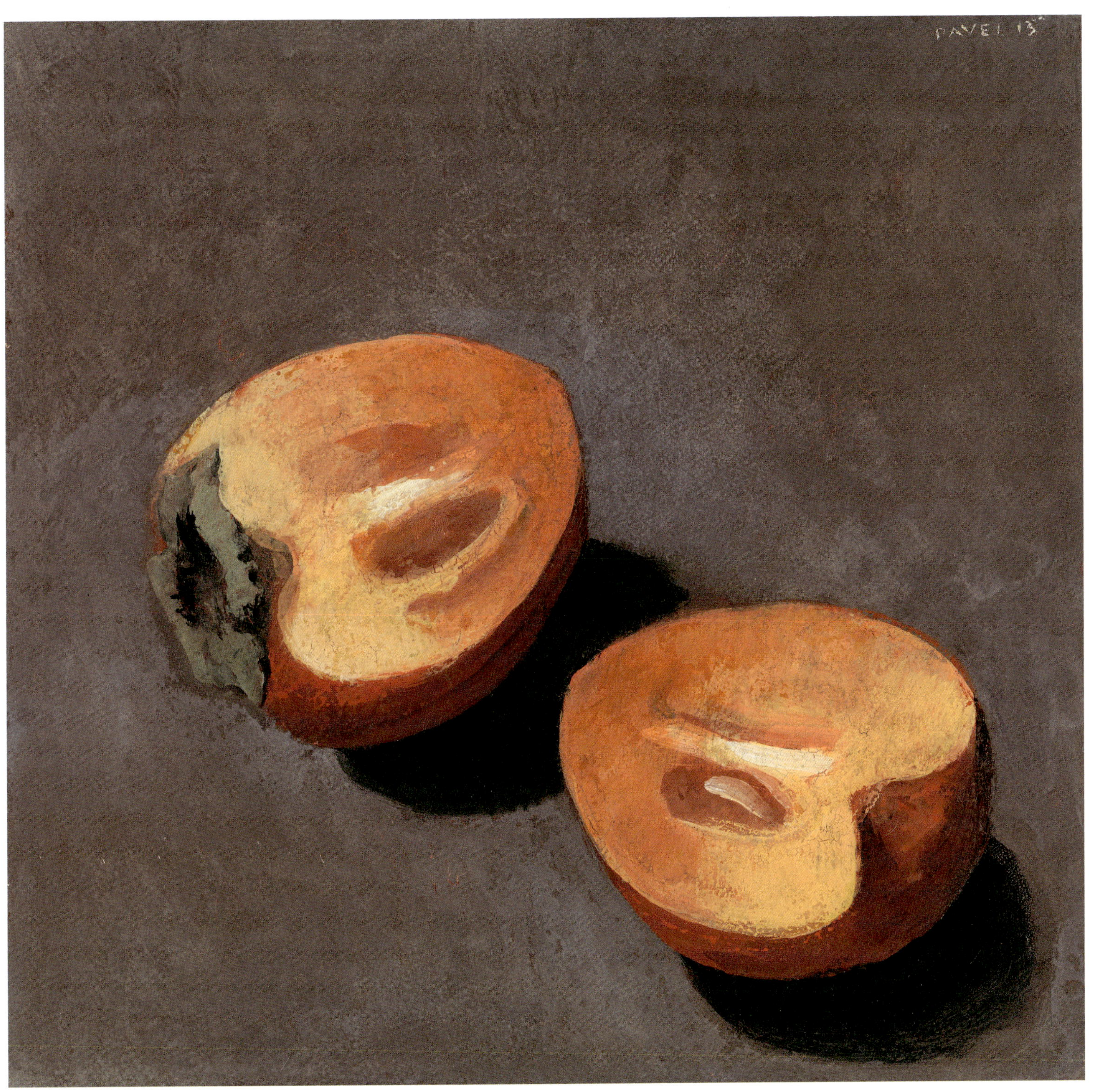
PAVEL 13

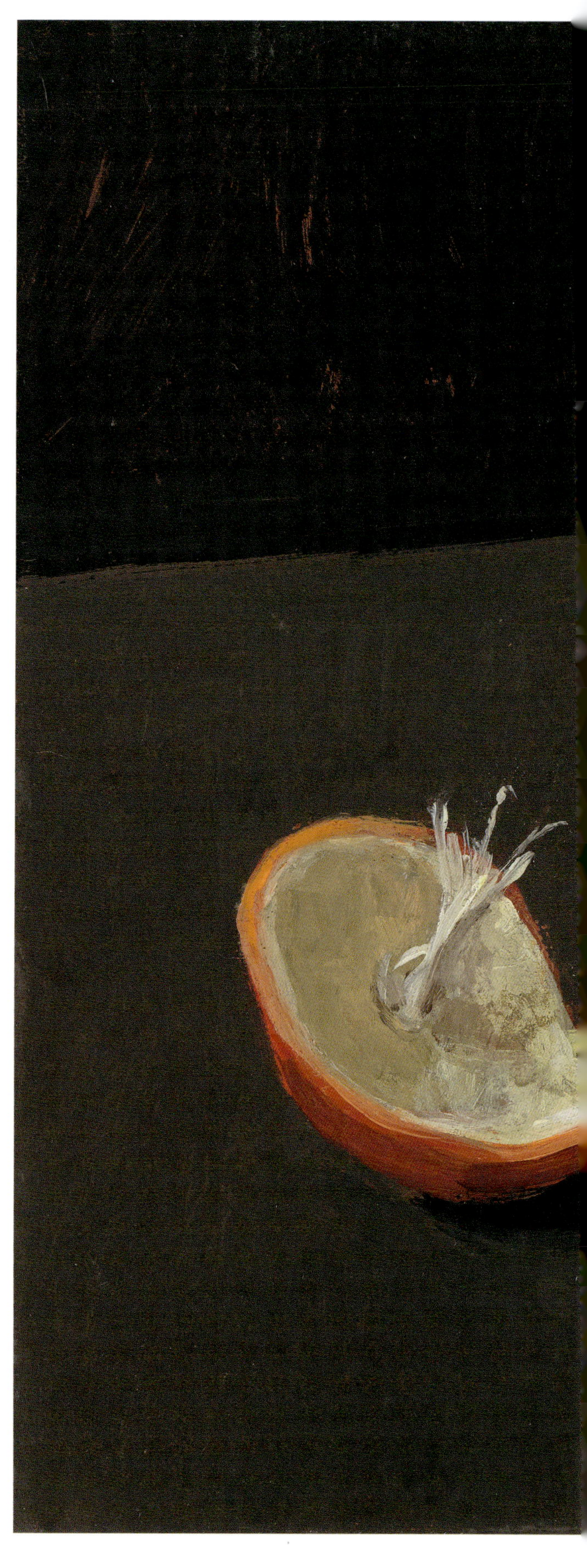

1972, **Tempera auf Hartfaser** / Tempera on hardboard, 30 × 40 cm, 2015

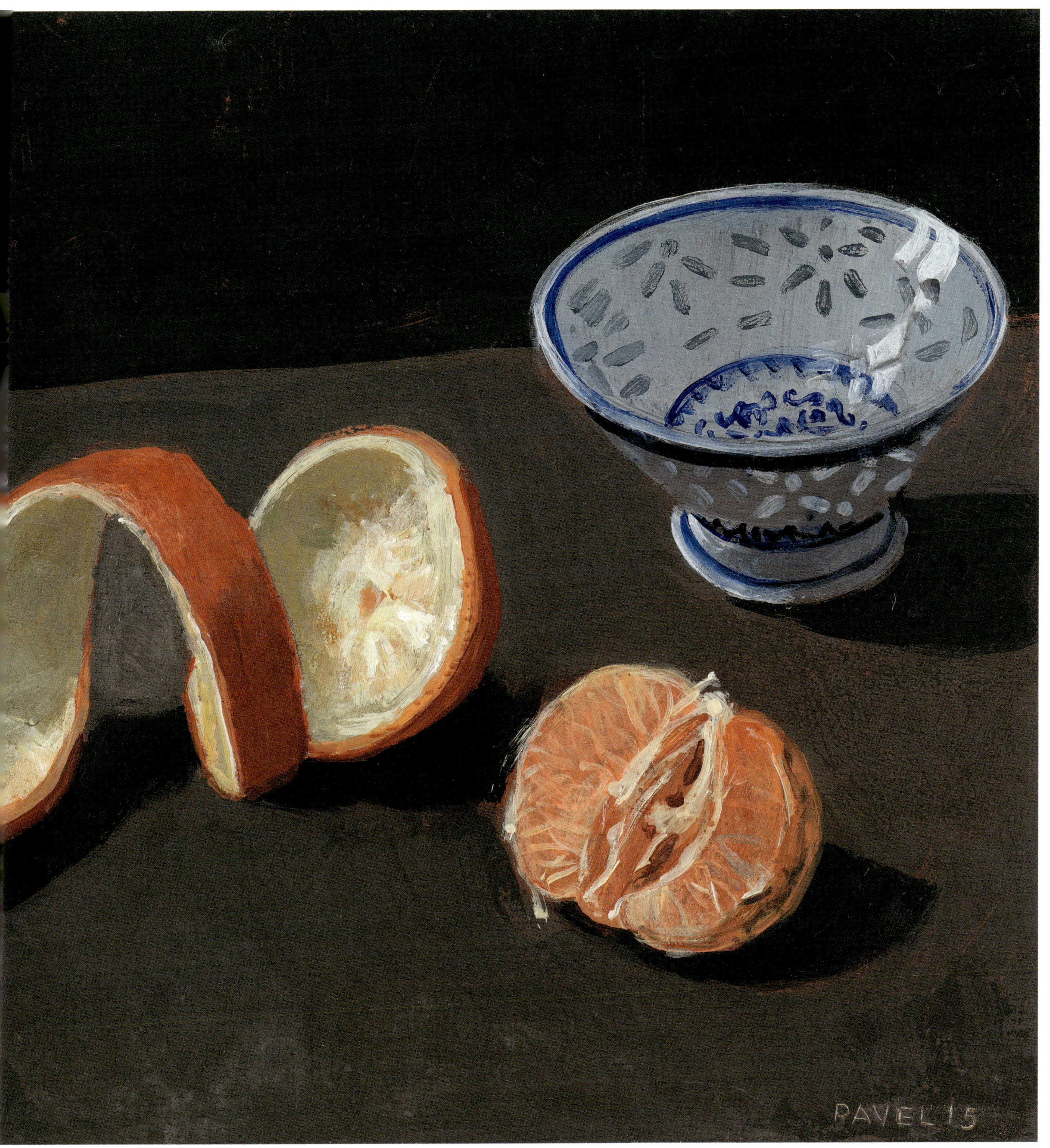
PAVEL 15

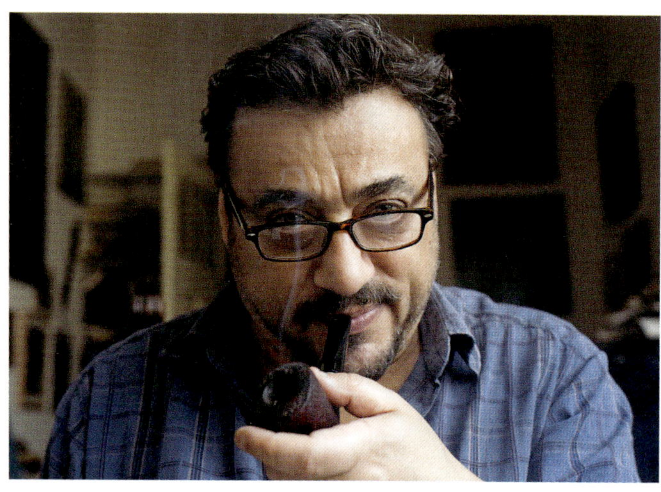

Biografie / Biography

1960	**geboren in Moskau** / Born in Moscow
1965	**Umzug der Familie nach Duschanbe, Tadschikistan** / Family moved to Dushanbe, Tajikistan
1978/79	**College of Art, Duschanbe** / College of Art, Dushanbe
1980	**Emigration** / Emigration
1980–1985	**Studium an der HdK, Berlin** / Studied at the University of the Arts, Berlin
1985	**Meisterschüler bei Prof. G. Bergmann** / Master student of Prof. G. Bergmann

Einzelausstellungen (Auswahl) / Solo exhibitions (selection)

Jüdisches Museum Berlin / Jewish Museum, Berlin
Felix-Nussbaum-Haus, Osnabrück
Moses Mendelssohn Akademie, Halberstadt
Osthaus Museum Hagen
Zitadelle Spandau, Berlin
Städtische Galerie »Fähre«, Bad Saulgau
Schloss Bonndorf

Vertreten durch / Represented by

Galerie KK, Essen
Galerie lorch + seidel contemporary, Berlin
Galerie Ewald Schrade, Karlsruhe + Schloss Mochental
Galerie Tobias Schrade, Ulm

Kontakt / Contact

Galerie KK Klaus Kiefer
infokk@t-online.de
www.galerie-kk.de

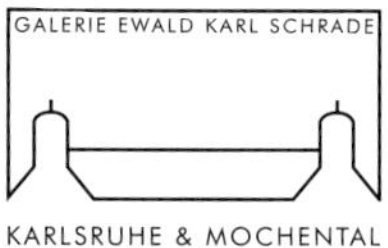

schrade@galerie-schrade.de
www.galerie-schrade.de

Impressum / Colophon

Hirmer Verlag GmbH
Nymphenburger Straße 84
80636 München

Hirmer Publishers GmbH
Nymphenburger Str. 84
80636 Munich
Germany

Übersetzung des Textes von Kay Heymer /
Translation of the text by Kay Heymer
Mason Ellis Murray
Fotos / Photography
Gunter Lepkowski, Berlin, und / *and*
Martina Strilic, Ulm
Gestaltung, Satz und Produktion /
Design, Typesetting and Production
Sabine Frohmader
Lithografie / Lithography
Reproline mediateam, Unterföhring
Druck und Bindung / Printed and bound by
Passavia Druckservice, Passau
Papier / Paper
LuxoArt Samt new 150 g/m²

Printed in Germany

Bibliografische Information der Deutschen Nationalbibliothek
Die Deutsche Nationalbibliothek verzeichnet diese Publikation in der Deutschen Nationalbibliografie; detaillierte bibliografische Daten sind im Internet über http://dnb.de abrufbar.
Bibliographic information published by the Deutsche Nationalbibliothek
The Deutsche Nationalbibliothek lists this publication in the Deutsche Nationalbibliografie; detailed bibliographic data are available in the Internet at http://dnb.de.

ISBN 978-3-7774-2447-7

www.hirmerverlag.de
www.hirmerpublishers.com

Abbildungen / Illustrations

Umschlagabbildung vorne /
Front cover illustration
1851, Tempera auf Hartfaser / *Tempera on hardboard,* ***30 × 30 cm, 2014***
Umschlagabbildung Rückseite /
Back cover illustration
1886, Tempera auf Hartfaser / *Tempera on hardboard,* ***30 × 30 cm, 2014***
Abbildung Seite 2 / page 2
1228, Öl auf Leinwand / *Oil on canvas,* ***50 × 60 cm, 2009***
Abbildung Seite 4 / page 4
1802, Tempera auf Hartfaser / *Tempera on hardboard,* ***30 × 30 cm, 2013, Detail***
Abbildung Seite 122 / page 122
Foto des Künstlers von Vladimir Sichov /
Photo of the artist by Vladimir Sichov

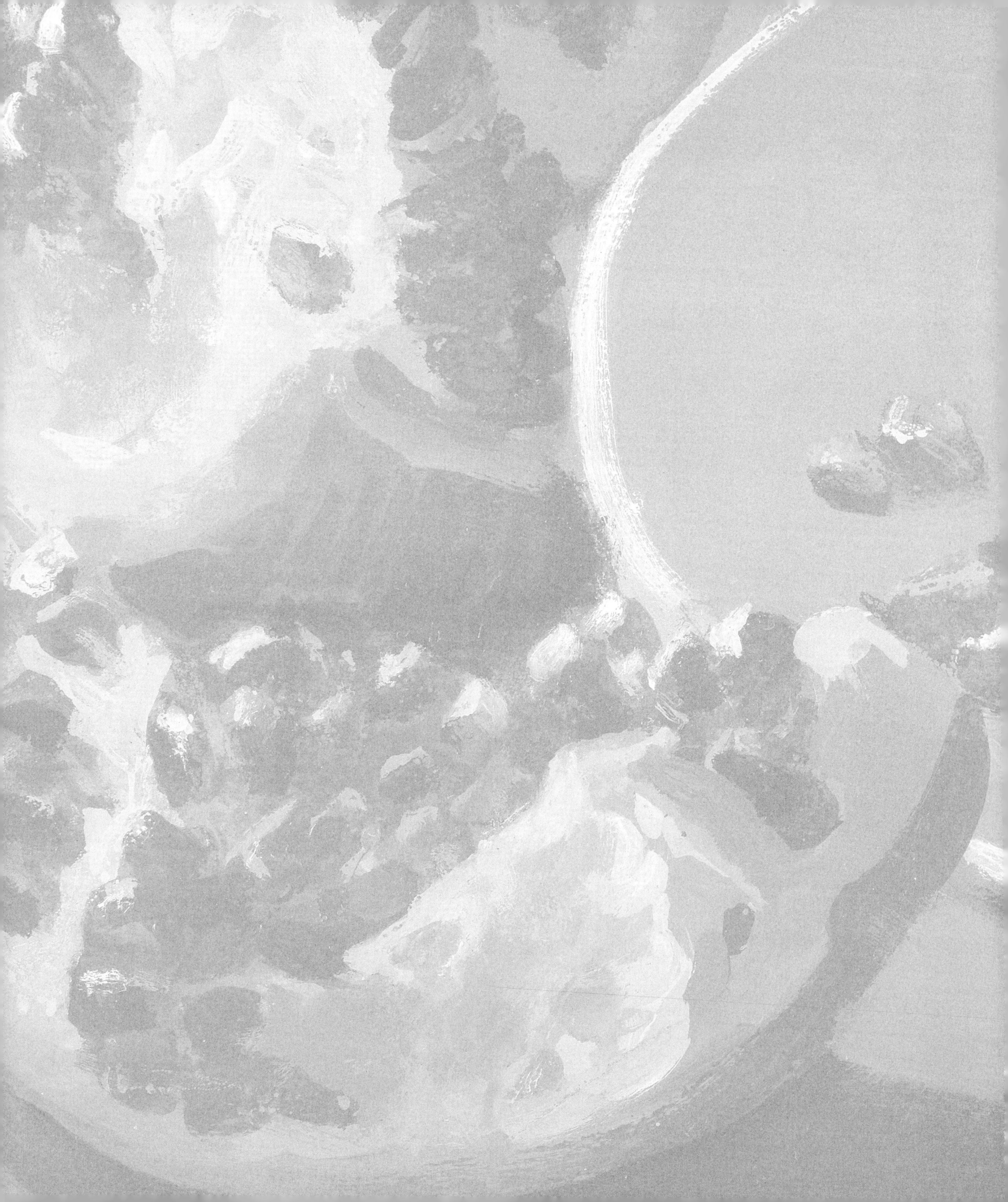